SOCCER LAWS
EXPLAINED

Photo: Phil Stephens

SOCCER LAWS
EXPLAINED

Stanley Lover

Foreword by
J S Blatter
General Secretary – FIFA

With
The Laws of the Game
and
**Decisions of the International
Football Association Board**
Reproduction authorised by
Fédération Internationale de Football Association
FIFA
(All rights reserved by FIFA)

Eric Dobby Publishing

Also by *Stanley Lover;*
Soccer Laws Illustrated
Soccer Match Control
Soccer Judge

Published by Eric Dobby Publishing Ltd,
12 Warnford Road, Orpington, Kent BR6 6LW.

A catalogue record for this book is available from the British Library

Typeset in 10pt on 13pt Garamond by Inforum, Rowlands Castle, Hants

Illustrations by Stanley Lover

Contents

Foreword

Sepp Blatter. Photo: FIFA

The title alone of this book guarantees its success. The followers of our sport are constantly increasing in number and are eager to enjoy it to the fullest.

Explaining the Laws in such a clear and simple way is not easy. This publication manages to do so and its future readers, which we hope will be numerous, will undoubtedly benefit in more ways than one from the new information gleaned from it.

J.S. Blatter
FIFA General Secretary

Introduction

Something strange was happening at the giant Workers' Stadium. Peking were playing Tientsin before 40,000 fans who applauded enthusiastically but the applause seemed to be related to a match being played somewhere else in China because it often occurred when there was no action on the field. Play had been stopped for a free-kick when an announcement was broadcast provoking appreciative reaction from the fans.

An interpreter explained the mystery by pointing to a person seated at a table close to the touch-line. "He is the person giving the commentary. He is one of our leading referees and is explaining the decisions of the match referee Dr Wong, who is a professor of physical culture."

As the game proceeded the interpreter gave a summary of the commentary:

"No. 6 obstructed an opponent. Dr Wong has awarded an indirect free-kick and is confirming the decision with one arm raised above his head."

"The goal was not allowed because Dr Wong noticed that No. 10 handled the ball. He has awarded a direct free-kick to Tientsin."

"Dr Wong has signalled permission for the Peking medical assistant to enter the field to examine the injury to No. 6. He has stopped his watch so that no playing time is lost."

"Off-side. No. 7 was in an off-side position at the moment the ball was passed towards him. The referee considered that he was interfering with play and has awarded an indirect free-kick to Peking. Notice again, the signal – one arm raised above the head."

"Although that was not an intentional foul Dr Wong considered that it was too dangerous to the opponent. Indirect free-kick."

There was no doubt that the fans welcomed this additional insight into the game as seen through the eyes of an expert. They understood why the match was stopped and the appropriate action required by the laws. Their appreciation was such that the match officials were applauded more than the players!

It is not practical to consider a similar commentary for all soccer games but the experience made the point that fans, and players, want to know more about what is happening in *their* match.

Many players will confess that they play through their soccer lives without giving much thought to the laws because the game is simple and it is the job of the referee to apply the laws. If it were a fact that players and spectators accepted referees' decisions without dissent this attitude would be reasonable but, in practice, much confusion and irritation are generated when perfectly sound decisions are misinterpreted due to lack of knowledge of the laws to which the game must be played. Players also miss the opportunity of achieving full potential by not appreciating how to use the laws to their advantage. For example, a forward with exciting talent for scoring goals loses a chance to demonstrate his skills every time he is penalised for off-side. On some occasions it is difficult to avoid being off-side but, with a clear understanding of why the law is there and how off-side can be avoided the player can improve his own performance and contribute more to the success of his team.

It is clearly sensible to advise all involved in soccer to read the Laws of the Game but to open the law book is to enter forbidding territory because of the dry-as-dust legal terminology which is necessary to bear credible translation into other languages. The official laws can bore all but the most dedicated student.

The purpose of the book is to open a new window on the Game of Soccer by providing an easy-to-read guide to the game itself, to how the laws were formulated, to discover the reason and wisdom behind formal phrases and the practical interpretations seen in every match.

After a brief review of the pleasures of playing and watching soccer, and a background to its laws, there follows an explanation of each law by way of an introduction to the official text.

Whatever your role and experience in the game the contents of this book are intended to add a new perspective to future matches in the form of your own commentary on the events of play as revealed to the 40,000 fans and players in the Workers' Stadium, Peking, China.

The magic of a ball. A friend for life

Acknowledgements

The author and publishers acknowledge, with pleasure, the support of FIFA in granting permission to reproduce the official Laws of the Game, approved signals and other material.

1

The game of soccer

Why soccer attracts millions

There has to be something really special about a game with 40 million players spread throughout 175 countries. A game which counts among its followers young and old, male and female, all creeds, classes, colours, nationalities and political persuasions. A game which touches the life of practically every person on this earth, in one way or another, when one tournament, the FIFA World Cup, comes to its climax.

What is so special about soccer? What makes it the world's most popular sport?

First things first. Why "soccer"? What does the name mean? Officially the game is "Association Football", being the description adopted in 1863 when a handful of clubs met in London to agree on a common set of rules of play. From this The Football Association was founded.

"Soccer" is a word attributed to Charles Wreford-Brown one of the game's early amateur gentlemen players. Known by friends as "Reefer" he was an outstanding sportsman. An England soccer international in the late 1890s "Reefer" Brown also played top-class rugby and cricket. When seasons overlapped he would play whichever sport pleased him. One day a friend asked, "Are you playing rugger today?". (Rugger was, and still is, another word for rugby football.) In reply "Reefer" Brown said, "No, I'm playing soccer", a play-word of "association". He could have said "footer", another popular description, but "soccer" has become established particularly in countries where other forms of football are played such as Rugby Union, Rugby League, American and Australian Rules Football.

The game of soccer was born out of an ancient communal ceremony where hundreds of participants engaged in a rough and tumble scramble for a ball with the object of moving it to a defined target. Other forms of ball games, practised in China, Greece, Italy, France, etc. have influenced the formation of the modern game of soccer.

Today's game is a joy to play because each player can demonstrate personal skills. It is a joy to watch because the ball is always visible and easy to follow.

While a formal game requires two teams of eleven players much fun can be had from kick-a-about games with fewer players.

Playing is appealing enough but soccer attracts non-players who enjoy the spectacle of colour, athleticism, constant ebb and flow of play, the heroes and the villains. Watchers become involved whether the game is at schoolboy level, in the park, or is part of the carnival atmosphere of a World Cup event. Deep passions are aroused as watchers share emotional ties with supporters of club or national teams.

Undoubtedly the players are the main attraction. With a ball they can thrill us with clever skills, breathtaking spontaneity, enviable agility. Exceptionally gifted players become soccer gods, their names inscribed in soccer history, each worshipped by successive generations of soccer folk.

A vital element to soccer's attraction, possibly *the* vital element, is the object used in the game – the ball. For what would a soccer god be without a ball? Just an ordinary human being!

Why should the ball be so significant? The laws require that, "the ball shall be spherical". A wise choice because a sphere is a psychological symbol having pleasant associations with the Earth, Sun and Moon. Spherical objects, chosen specially to represent the powers of the Sun, have been used for centuries in rituals to ensure good harvests.

Soccer is a form of tribal ceremony very evident at important matches involving thousands of supporters. Tribal customs include collective chants, wearing good luck symbols, mass gestures and, in some countries, the performing of witchcraft to keep away evil spirits.

Almost from birth we develop an hypnotic attraction for a ball, one of our first toys. Present any child with a ball and the reaction is immediate – a smile. An inanimate object and yet it comes alive with a slight touch. It will rarely be still, being pushed, rolled, bounced, thrown or kicked into dynamic action. A ball is smooth, comfortable to hold and becomes a friend for life.

Games with a ball have been around since the beginning of time. Playing with one combines the fascination of a sphere with an expression of physical ability. The ball reproduces and measures personal skill.

The game of soccer is special because it unites these charms into a disciplined sporting contest.

Football in The Middle Ages: Entertainment of the common people, a noisy tough tussle in the streets

How soccer is played

Before discussing the laws which regulate play it may be helpful to outline the object of the game and how it is played.

A game of soccer is a match between two teams, each having eleven players, with the object of moving a ball between two targets (goals). The players may use any part of the body, except the hands, to control or propel the ball.

One player of each team is designated as a keeper of the goal (goalkeeper) and may use the hands to prevent the ball from passing through the goal. Goalkeepers wear colours different from the other players so that it is clear who may handle the ball.

The team which makes the highest number of goals wins the match. If there are no goals, or an equal goal count, the match is a draw.

Game rules specify the size and markings of the field of play, components required, time limits, procedures and disciplines to be followed.

There is no fixed formation of players. The goalkeeper, because of his role, stays near to the goal but outfield players have freedom of movement. According to preference, ability or tactics, players adopt certain positions in defence, mid-field or attack. They may interchange positions freely although in most levels of soccer some degree of specialisation develops.

The passing game

The powerful kick

A fair challenge for possession of the ball

A fair tackle playing the ball

Control

The dribble

The heading duel

The spectacular volley

Heading for goal

On the field each team is limited to eleven players but an additional five players may be nominated as possible substitutes. Not more than two may be used under the rules of a competition but for other games a maximum of five may be allowed.

When the ball is in play every player has the right to challenge for possession. This may involve varying degrees of physical contact between opponents. This is allowed providing it is fair and not dangerous.

Individual skills in playing with the ball, such as control, running, kicking, heading, passing it to a team mate, contribute to the overall team effort in moving the ball towards and through the opponents goal.

A neutral person, a referee, is on the field to apply the procedures and disciplines required by the rules of play. He may be supported by two officials, each carrying a flag and patrolling a touch-line, to assist with decisions relating to the ball crossing the boundary lines or off-side. The referee controls play with a whistle and arm signals.

The pleasure of playing soccer

The foregoing outline indicates the simplicity of the game. It is also an emotional experience. For the player, anticipation and excitement of an enjoyable activity starts when a soccer game is announced, be it hours, days or weeks in advance. The journey to the field, meeting team mates, engaging in soccer talk in a friendly atmosphere make for a special occasion.

Changing from everyday clothes into colourful soccer strip is like taking on a new personality, satisfying a natural desire to dress up to play a role. In the dressing-room a unique mixture of sights, sounds and smells sets nerves tingling similar to the pre-curtain tension experienced by stage artists.

Although a close comradeship exists some players may show signs of acute nervous anxiety. One of the world's greatest players, Sir Stanley Matthews, who played professional soccer from 16 to 50 years of age, admitted to being physically sick before some of his matches.

Running onto a soccer field, particularly in front of many fans, is another special moment although it may add to anxiety. However, all pre-match nerves are calmed at the first touch of the ball. Concentration can now be focussed on the game ahead.

During the match soccer pleasure mounts with increasing mental and physical exertions needed to solve problems arising from constantly changing action. All attention and movement is centred on the ball. It seems to radiate invisible signals to the players like expanding ripples caused by a stone dropping into a calm lake. Each player interprets the signals according to individual ability while being conscious of his role as a member of a team. Instant decisions are necessary after assessing the best position to meet the next phase of play, whether to move close to an opponent to reduce his effectiveness or to go for the ball, to cover a team mate, how best to control the ball coming fast at an awkward angle with only a split second before contact. When in possession a quick evaluation of options available is needed before deciding to run with the ball, move it to a team mate, try to pass an opponent or take a shot at goal.

Emotions fluctuate with successes and failures, from great elation when your team scores to despair when a goal is lost. The end of the match brings congratulations, commiserations, and an inquest into the main events of play, all in an atmosphere charged with another unique mixture of sights, sounds and smells.

Whatever the result leaving for home gives time for reflection leading to a degree of satisfaction in having taken part in a sporting contest, sharing an emotional experience with friends and counting the days to the next match.

The pleasure of watching soccer

Soccer games have always attracted spectators whether in the form of one man and his dog strolling in the park or the estimated 200,000

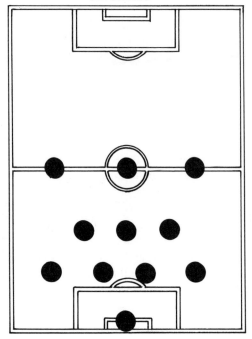

The 4–3–3 system

fanatics who stormed the Wembly Stadium gates to see the 1923 FA Cup Final between West Ham United and Bolton Wanderers.

In the first century of its existence soccer has been well supported by millions attending matches, mostly under primitive conditions. The supporter has often been treated as a necessary evil even when paying for the privilege of standing on cramped terraces exposed to the worst of winter elements. Even today references to spectators in soccer laws are concerned with "interference with the play, misconduct and misdemeanours".

One, seemingly grudging, recognition that spectators may wish to enjoy the game appears at the end of a note in which referees are advised not to constantly stop play "for trifling or doubtful offences" as this can cause bad feeling among players and "spoils the pleasure of spectators".

Soccer is now being presented as an entertainment package with Olympic-style ceremonies and show-biz sparkle to keep fans happy enough to behave themselves. A remarkable expansion of televised soccer has attracted vast audiences to the point where more people

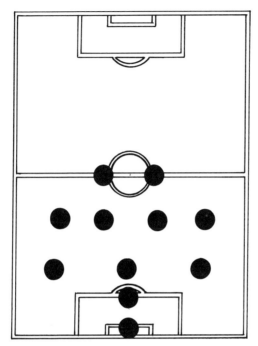

The 'sweeper' system with 3–4–2
No fixed formation of players. These are just two of several combinations with specific
tasks in defence, mid-field and attack

watch soccer from the comfort of their homes than from the sidelines.

The degree of pleasure to be gained from watching the game itself varies according to knowledge and experience. Newcomers may be content to be carried along with the general atmosphere created by a group of enthusiastic sportsmen chasing a ball. For the very sound reasons already given, relating to the magnetic attraction of a ball, newcomers will find it dificult to take their eyes off the ball and think that the object of the game is to kick it aimlessly up and down the field until someone puts it into a goal. Well, that's not a bad start. With more exposure to the game comes knowledge and more pleasure.

Players, and ex-players, get their pleasure from watching based on an inner knowledge of "can do, have done". They identify with the physical effort, the skills and techniques. Every touch of the ball has a personal meaning whether it be instant control, an accurate pass, a shot at goal or, even, a miss-kick! Many can appreciate the cut and thrust of tactical play,

Sir Stanley Matthews, 'The Prince of Dribblers'. A world professional star from 16 to 50 years of age

watching for unusual moves to highlight each match.

The watcher who sees the most is the soccer expert, the connoisseur, who has spent a lifetime in the game. Starting as a player then developing knowledge and experience by serving as a coach, referee, administrator, writer, or a combination of several functions, the connoisseur takes in the whole scenario of every second. He will start by sizing up the pre-match factors which may influence the play. He will know the importance of the result for both teams whether it be to gain promotion or avoid relegation in a league, or advance to the next stage of a special competition. He will know the abilities of the players selected and will form an idea of how they will be used tactically.

The connoisseur will look for any abnormal conditions which may affect the play. The size of the field and state of the playing surface, the temperature, position and strength of the sun, wind, rain, or other adverse conditions will provide clues.

For the connoisseur a soccer match is like a game of chess with human beings as pieces deciding their own moves to mount attacks, centrally, along the sidelines or diagonals. He will look for defence strategy, counter-attacks, the key players, the weak links, positional intelligence. He will assess the options available to the player in possession, judge decision making ability, ball control skills, timing of challenges.

The connoisseur quickly identifies the real stars, potential troublemakers, the weak referee. He calculates the outcome of each phase of play, revising forecasts as the tactical scene changes.

The connoisseur acts out the roles of the player, the coach, referee and the fan. He can be seen participating with reactive body language to resist a crunching tackle, swaying to deceive an opponent or thrusting his head forward to nod the ball into goal.

For him the game is much more than moving a ball between two goals, it is total immersion in the charms of what he calls "The Beautiful Game".

Women in soccer, the fashion in the first match played by the British Ladies Football Club was nightcaps, skirts, shinguards and heavy boots (1895)

Soccer for women

"The Beautiful Game" counts among its admirers millions of women with over one million registered players.

Women have played soccer since the 14th century but regular teams began to appear only 500 years later. In today's world women's soccer is highly organised with established leagues and international tournaments. Administrators of women's soccer have battled incessantly for official

The World number one woman player, Michelle Akers-Stahl, star of the USA team which won the historic First Women's World Championship, China, 1991. Photo: Phil Stevens

recognition and their efforts were finally rewarded when FIFA decided, in 1991, to form a special committee responsible for women's soccer on a global basis.

A new page in soccer history was turned when, in the same year, FIFA organised the first FIFA World Championship for Women's Football, in China. The tournament attracted huge interest after it was seen to be played to a surprising level of skill with only slight differences in the laws concerning the size of the ball and duration of play.

An astute move by FIFA because today's women soccer players will be the mothers of tomorrow's soccer children, educated to appreciate the special qualities of the game.

2
Background to soccer law

The role of soccer law

The original role of soccer law was to provide a uniform code of rules for several similar ball games played in universities, clubs and colleges during the 19th century. A simple role but many years were to pass before a universal code was agreed. Successive generations of legislators have refined its text without changing basic principles or ethics.

Today the role of soccer law is just about perfect. It provides a simple game which can be played within the physical limits of any person. It can be played anywhere with inexpensive equipment, with time and space for players to develop individual skills inside a team sport, in a healthy environment and be attractive enough to arouse the passions of millions of spectators.

The game of soccer is very special because its laws have very special qualities.

Need for a common code

Modern soccer can be played by millions but when the founders of the game met to decide on a common code of play they were concerned only to satisfy the needs of a few English public schools and universities. During the early 1800s these important institutions combined sports with moral instruction to prepare future leaders of the nation's business, government and military services, for the responsibilities ahead.

Football was one of the sports chosen to harden bodies, test courage, develop self-discipline and promote sound ethics. Each school had its own form of game according to the facilities available. The London schools of Charterhouse and Westminster, restricted to play in small cloisters, favoured a dribbling game. Cheltenham and Rugby used the space of open fields to play a more scrambling game similar to early

The great influence of public school football. Captured here in a match between Charterhouse and Old Cartusian Internationals in 1892. Note the referee in white and an umpire in formal dress and school cap. The sixth player from the left is 'Reefer' Brown, who is thought to have invented the word 'soccer'

mob-street football.

The need for a common method of play arose when students passed on to university. Attempts to organise football games ended in chaos because the undergraduates played to the rules of their own public school. Thus it was that a committee was set up at Cambridge University to devise a game which would incorporate the best features of the variations practised by the public schools.

The main issue was to decide between moving the ball by kicking and dribbling or running with it and allowing physical assaults on opponents to gain possession. The vote went in favour of the former probably because of the argument that mature players, in professions with heavy responsibilities, would be discouraged from playing for fear of serious injury.

Although the first common rules, known as the Cambridge Rules, were intended to resolve an internal problem they were to become a major source of reference when a universal code was adopted in 1863 by the newly formed Football Association.

Football had now turned away from the roughness, violence and confusion of the mob-style methods to a more open game giving the players opportunities to display skills with the ball and to encourage tactical development in team play.

Organisation and skill are the main differences between ancient and modern forms of soccer. We shall see how current laws spell out the simple basics required to organise a game and how players are able to demonstrate their skills.

Who controls the laws?

Tradition is important in soccer. The game has grown to global popularity due not only to the wisdom of the founders of an attractive sport but also to the spreading of its virtues to many countries by British soldiers, sailors, teachers, industrialists, etc.

The British contribution is recognised in the composition of the body which controls soccer law, the International Football Association Board. The four British associations of England, Scotland, Ireland, and Wales, are partners with FIFA (Fédération Internationale de Football Association) in forming the Board. FIFA is a federation of over 170 national football associations. Its objects are to promote and control the game, to foster friendly relations, to prevent discrimination and to decide differences

RULES

Passed at International Conference held in London, June, 1886.

1.—That this Board shall be called "THE INTERNATIONAL FOOTBALL ASSOCIATION BOARD," and shall be composed of two representatives from each of the four national associations.

2.—That the Board shall meet each year in the month of June at the invitation of each of the national associations in the order of seniority.

3.—That at such meeting one of the representatives of the association convening the same shall preside, and the other shall act as secretary.

4.—That the minute-book of the meetings shall ·be fully entered up by the secretary, and shall be forwarded to the association next in turn before the 1st of January ensuing.

5.—That business shall not be proceeded with unless a majority of the associations be represented.

6.—That resolutions shall not be adopted unless agreed to by three-fourths of those present ; but in the case of alterations of laws of the game, a unanimous vote shall be necessary.

7.—That the Board shall discuss and decide proposed alterations in the laws of the game and generally any matters affecting Association football in its international relations

8.—That the committees of the various national associations shall forward in writing, on or before 1st February each year, to the secretary ot the association entitled to convene the next meeting, any suggestions or alterations deemed desirable, which shall be printed and distributed on or before 1st March, for consideration at the annual general meetings of the association.

9.—That decisions of this Board shall be at once binding on all the associations, and no alterations in the laws of the game made by any association shall be valid until accepted by this Board.

The next International Conference will be held at Glasgow in June, 1887.

First Rules of the International Football Board. Photo: FIFA

which may arise between national associations.

The International Board meets annually to discuss and decide proposed alterations to the Laws of the Game and any other matters referred to it by its members. Since its formation in 1886 by the four British associations joined in 1913 by FIFA, the International Board has been extremely conservative when considering the many suggestions received each year. Its policy is to make changes only when there is positive evidence that change is necessary.

In recent years the IB has amended certain laws to combat undesirable trends in the game which have put undue emphasis on defensive tactics and excess physical contact. The role of the goalkeeper has caused concern resulting in restrictions intended to make the ball more available to outfield players. Time-wasting, violent tackles, deliberate foul play and handling of the ball, now incur severe punishments. Various experiments have been authorised to test ideas for changes but results have to be very conclusive before the IB will agree to any modification.

Changes can only occur when agreed by at least three-quarters of the total of eight votes held in the proportion of one each for the four British Associations and four votes for FIFA. Effectively there can be no change without the support of FIFA.

Deliberations of the IB are notified to all national associations in the form of an amendment to law, a decision which clarifies a certain aspect of a law, instructions, or advice, together with reasons and hoped-for effect. Much care is taken to compile announcements in formal English capable of accurate translation into all world languages. Sometimes it is difficult to avoid a legalistic style which makes for heavy reading – a major reason for the need of this book!

Interpretations and clarifications of the laws are published in the form of questions and answers. These deal with official queries submitted by national associations and represent soccer case law. A selection of questions and official answers is included at the end of this book.

As guardians of the law members of the International Board are required to exercise practical wisdom in weighing up the probable consequences of proposed changes. They are concerned not only with technicalities of play but also with preserving the moral character-forming qualities intended by the founders of the game.

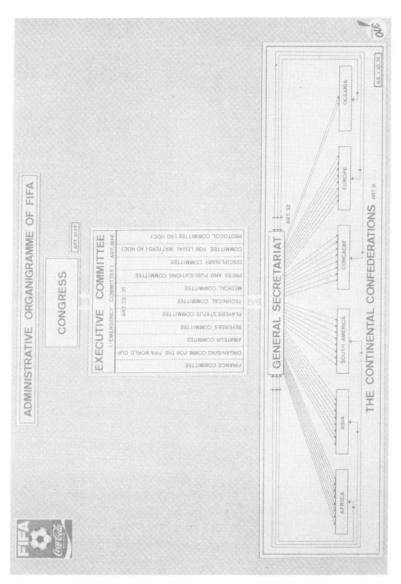

Organisation of FIFA. Photo: FIFA

3
Soccer Laws Explained

Definition

"Law; a rule prescribed by authority", is a very dull definition in any context. There seems little connection between this word and the exciting, vibrant, colourful spectacle of a game of soccer and yet, without law, or rules, there can be no guiding principles, no organisation, no discipline, no control, no interest, no fun, and no game.

The fact that soccer has intoxicated the world proves that the formula to which it is played, i.e. the laws of the game, must have some special qualities. We shall see how simple these qualities are and how they appear in every kick, and every facet of play.

Construction of soccer law

We have seen how modern soccer emerged out of ancient forms of ball games because the confusion of different interpretations spelt out the need for a common formula. The original laws, adopted in 1863, comprised just fourteen short paragraphs and eight definitions. Today, they have expanded to seventeen laws of clauses and sub-clauses plus 82 Decisions (of The International Board). Add 153 official Questions and Answers; numerous examples of Off-side; Instructions for the taking of Kicks from the Penalty-spot to decide special matches; Instructions and Guidance for Referees and Linesmen; The Diagonal System of Control; Signals of the match officials; Instructions for an extra official; and we see the task of administrators to cover every eventuality and the problem of achieving total comprehension.

Basic principles

Despite the formidable nature of the mass of law and appendices the whole becomes easy to understand when the principles on which it is

I.

The maximum **length of the ground** shall be 200 yards, the maximum **breadth** shall be 100 yards, the length and breadth shall be marked off with flags; and the **goal** shall be defined by two upright posts, 8 yards apart, without any tap or bar across them.

II.

The Game shall be commenced by a **place kick** from the centre of the ground by the side winning the toss, the other side shall not approach within 10 yards of the ball until it is kicked off. After a goal is won the losing side shall be entitled to kick off.

III.

The two sides shall change goals after each goal is won.

IV.

A goal shall be won when the ball passes over the space between the goal post (at whatever height), not being thrown, knocked on, or carried.

V.

When the ball is in **touch** the first player who touches it shall kick or throw it from the point on the boundary line where it left the ground, in a direction at right angles with the boundary line.

VI.

A player shall be **out of play** immediately he is in front of the ball, and must return behind the ball as soon as possible. If the ball is kicked past a player by his own side, he shall not touch or kick it or advance until one of the other side has first kicked it or one of his own side on a level with or in front of him has been able to kick it.

VII.

In case the ball goes behind the goal line, if a player on the side to whom the goal belongs first touches the ball, one of his side shall be entitled to a free kick from the goal line at the point opposite the place where the ball shall be touched. If a player of the opposite side first touches the ball, one of his side shall be entitled to a free kick from a point 15 yards outside the goal line, opposite the place where the ball is touched.

The Laws of the Game as they were finally adopted by The
Football Association in December 1863. Photo: FIFA

VIII.

If a player makes a **fair catch** he shall be entitled to a **free kick**, provided l claims it by making a mark with his heel at once; and in order to take such kick he ma go as far back as he pleases, and no player on the opposite side shall advance beyond h mark until he has kicked.

IX.

A player shall be entitled to run with the ball towards his adversaries' goal if l makes a fair catch, or catches the ball on the first bound; but in the case of a fair catch, he makes his mark, he shall not then run.

X.

If any player shall run with the ball towards his adversaries' goal, any player on th opposite side shall be at liberty to charge, hold, trip, or hack him, or to wrest the ball fro him; but no player shall be held and hacked at the same time.

XI.

Neither tripping or hacking shall be allowed, and no player shall use his hand r elbows to hold or push his adversary, except in the case provided for by Law X.

XII.

Any player shall be allowed to charge another, provided they are both in active play. A player shall be allowed to charge if even he is out of play.

XIII.

A player shall be allowed to throw the ball or pass it to another if he make a fai catch, or catches the ball on the first bound.

XIV.

No player shall be allowed to wear projecting nails, iron plates, or gutta percha he soles or heels of his boots.

DEFINITION OF TERMS.

A Place Kick—Is a Kick at the Ball while it is on the ground, in any position which the Kicker may choose to place it.

A Free Kick—Is the privilege of Kicking the Ball, without obstruction, in such manner as the Kicker may think fit.

A Fair Catch—Is when the Ball is Caught, after it has touched the person of an Adversary or has been kicked, knocked on, or thrown by an Adversary, and before it has touched the ground or one of the Side catching it; but if the Ball is kicked from out of touch, or from behind goal line, a fair Catch cannot be made.

Hacking—Is kicking an Adversary on the front of the leg, below the knee.

Tripping—Is throwing an Adversary by the use of the legs without the hands, and without hacking or charging.

Charging—Is attacking an Adversary with the shoulder, chest, or body, without using the hands or legs.

Knocking on—Is when a Player strikes or propels the Ball with his hands, arms or body, without kicking or throwing it.

Holding—Includes the obstruction of a Player by the hand or any part of the arm below the elbow.

Touch—Is that part of the field, on either side of the ground, which is beyond the line of flags.

based are clear, i.e. the spirit behind the written word. These are simply equality, safety and enjoyment.

Equality
Every player is entitled to an equal opportunity to demonstrate personal skills. The laws provide protection for players of all abilities by restricting the degree of physical contact when contesting possession of the ball.

Safety
To enable players to engage in a healthy sport all elements of danger are strictly controlled.

Enjoyment
To promote maximum enjoyment of the game all who take part are required to observe an honourable code of discipline and fair play.

Law groups

Before getting to the detail of each law there are logical relationships and groupings which can be stated as follows (law numbers in brackets):

Components:	Field of Play (I) – Ball (II) – Players (III) – Players' Equipment (IV)
Control:	Referees (V) – Linesmen (VI)
Game rules:	Duration (VII) – Start of Play (VIII) – Ball In and Out of Play (IX) – Method of Scoring (X)
Technical:	Off-side (XI)
Discipline:	Fouls and Misconduct (XII)
Restarts:	Free-kicks (XIII) – Penalty-kick (XIV) – Throw-in (XV) – Goal-kick (XVI) – Corner-kick (XVII)

In the next section the official Laws of the Game are published with an introduction to each of the groups noted above. Before the formal text of the law and International Board Decisions appears a commentary on the most important points of each law.

How to study the laws

The degree of knowledge you wish to acquire from a study of the laws depends on your interest or role in the game. A referee needs to study every word and know its interpretation whereas a player, coach, administrator, journalist or fan, can ignore much detail such as dimensions and technical specifications.

Whatever your interest you can obtain the most value from the time devoted to study if you establish priorities:

1. First priority – what you must know: basic facts of each law – its function (see groups) – why the game is stopped – punishment – how the game is restarted, etc.
2. Second priority – what you should know: relevant decisions – examples of special situations.
3. Third priority – matters of interest: cases from questions and answers.

The laws are formal and flexible. Formality of procedure or action is usually denoted by the words "shall be" or "must be". "The game *shall be* restarted . . .", "substitutes *must be* chosen from . . .", are examples. Flexibility is allowed for friendly matches (e.g. number of substitutes), players of school-age, veteran and women players (size of ball, duration of game, etc.).

National associations are permitted certain discretion, e.g. minimum number of players in a team, and some special rules apply for international matches, e.g. size of field.

There is much reason and wisdom within the laws. The basic principles of equality, safety and enjoyment become evident if each statement is questioned with the key word "WHY?". Why must the field be of oblong shape? Why must the ball be spherical? Why must opponents remain at least ten yards from the ball at free-kicks? Why off-side?

To analyse the content of each law in this manner puts a fresh meaning on that dull word "law" because we can appreciate the intentions of the founders, followed by successive generations of legislators, to make the game simple and enjoyable with the emphasis on preserving the moral character forming-qualities of a healthy sport played with passion while respecting the spirit of fair play.

4
Laws of the Game

I   – **The Field of Play**
II   – **The Ball**
III – **Number of Players**
IV   – **Players' Equipment**
V   – **Referees**
VI   – **Linesmen**
VII – **Duration of the Game**
VIII – **The Start of Play**
IX   – **Ball In and Out of Play**
X   – **Method of Scoring**
XI   – **Off-Side**
XII – **Fouls and Misconduct**
XIII – **Free-Kick**
XIV – **Penalty-Kick**
XV   – **Throw-In**
XVI – **Goal-Kick**
XVII – **Corner-Kick**

Notes

Subject to the agreement of the National Association concerned and
provided the principles of these Laws are maintained, the Laws may
be modified in their application for matches for players of under 16
years of age, for women's football and for veterans' football (over
35 years). Any or all of the following modifications are permissible:
(a) size of the field of play;
(b) size, weight and material of the ball;
(c) width between the goal-posts and height of the cross-bar from
    the ground;
(d) the duration of the periods of play;
(e) number of substitutions.
Further modifications are only possible with the consent of the
International Football Association Board.

Notes

Further modifications are only permissible with the consent of the International Football Association Board.

Reproduction of the Laws of the Game and Decisions of the International Football Association Board authorised by the Fédération Internationale de Football Association FIFA.

5
Components

I   – **The Field of Play**
II – **The Ball**
III – **Number of Players**
IV – **Players' Equipment**

Players, ball, space

Players, ball and space are the three essential elements of every soccer game. For organised matches the first four laws prescribe the detail of each element.

Law I – The Field of Play

This is the stage upon which all soccer artists perform their skills. Both teams have equal territory to defend on a field large enough to provide ample space for twenty-two players and yet not too large to demand excessive physical effort.

While the areas marked within the boundary lines have fixed sizes there is much latitude allowed in the length and breadth. This is particularly useful where playing areas are restricted, e.g. public parks. More fields can be accommodated giving more people the opportunity to play the game.

The goal-lines are self-explanatory, being where the goals are placed, but why are the sidelines named "touch-lines"? The name is a survivor from the original laws of 1863. When the ball crossed the side boundary line the first player to "touch" the ball was then entitled to kick or throw it back into play.

Every soccer field must be longer than it is wide because an oblong-shape channels the flow of play between the two target goals. This simple requirement contributes towards the interest and enjoyment of the

Why the law requires corner-posts to be a minimum of 5 feet (1.50 metres)

game.

Safety factors for the players include a minimum height of 5 feet for the flagpost, having a non-pointed top, and no V-shaped rut markings which could easily injure ankles and legs.

Flag-posts at the half-way line are optional being a legacy from original laws which did not require a half-way line. They are, however, compulsory at the corner-areas to help decide whether the ball has crossed the goal-line or touch-line.

The World Cup Final in 1974, between West Germany and Holland, nearly started without corner-posts. The English referee, Jack Taylor, was about to blow his whistle when he realised that the posts had not been replaced after the field had been used for the pre-match ceremony. His alertness avoided an embarrassing incident.

Field markings need not be of a special colour – just "distinctive". For important matches, particularly those shown on TV, we have become used to seeing white lines on beautifully manicured green-grassed fields but blue or red markings on a snow covered surface are quite acceptable.

Target goals are of a size which demand skill from attacking players to put a ball into them and from a goalkeeper to keep it out. Goal-nets may

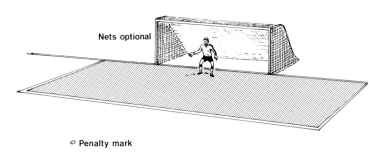

Goal and goal-area

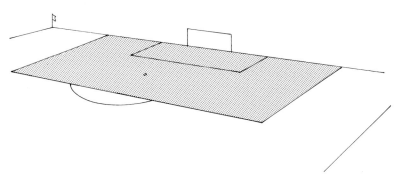

Penalty-area

be attached to the goals but they are not obligatory thus avoiding an additional financial burden on many thousands of amateur clubs.

The Goal-area is a zone of protection for goalkeepers against unfair physical contact from opponents. It is also the area from which goal-kicks are taken.

The Penalty-area is a vital zone for two reasons. The goalkeeper is the only player allowed to handle the ball within its boundaries, subject to certain restraints described later, and all defending players must be careful to avoid committing certain offences which can result in a severe punishment – a Penalty-kick – with a 90% chance of a goal being scored.

Two arcs, added to the penalty-areas, serve to mark a 10 yards (9.15 metres) distance from the penalty-mark which must be observed by players as is explained in the penalty-kick law (Law XIV).

The centre-circle serves the same purpose, at a Place-kick, where opponents must remain outside of the circle until the ball is kicked into play

(Law VIII).

When the ball crosses a boundary line play stops and is restarted by a Throw-in (Law XV), a Goal-kick (Law XVI) or a Corner-kick (Law XVII).

Wisely the law does not specify the surface on which soccer is played. The choice is unlimited although unwritten considerations are that the chosen surface does not present undue danger to the players and that the game is not brought into disrepute by being played on a surface which denies skilful play, e.g. on a waterlogged or ice-covered field.

It is one of the duties of the referee to inspect the field and equipment before every game in good time to have any faulty items corrected.

Although not mentioned in soccer law the welfare and security of spectators must be considered particularly where large numbers are expected. Such matters concern possible risk of encroachment onto the field to interfere with play or to escape from incidents off the field. For Football League matches referees are instructed to inspect the area surrounding the field including exits, fences, etc.

Several tragic incidents, which have occurred in a number of countries, have imposed these precautions and placed an onerous responsibility on administrators, team officials, referees, players and spectators.

LAW I
The Field of Play

The field of play and appurtenances shall be as shown in the following plan:*

(1) **Dimensions.** The field of play shall be rectangular, its length being not more than 130 yards nor less than 100 yards and its breadth not more than 100 yards nor less than 50 yards. (In international matches the length shall be not more than 120 yards nor less than 110 yards and the breadth not more than 80 yards nor less than 70 yards.) The length shall in all cases exceed the breadth.

(2) **Marking.** The field of play shall be marked with dis-

* see next page

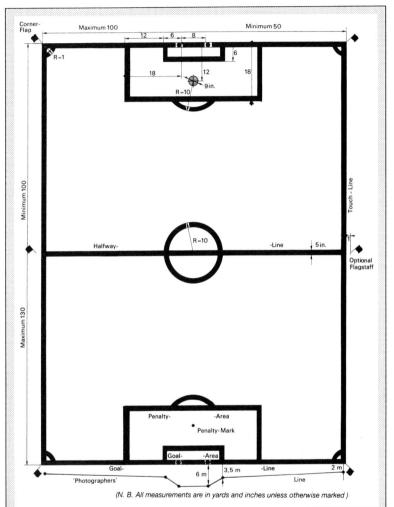

(N. B. All measurements are in yards and inches unless otherwise marked.)

tinctive lines, not more than 5 inches in width (not by a V-shaped rut) in accordance with the plan, the longer boundary lines being called the touch-lines and the shorter the goal-lines. A flag on a post not less than 5 ft. high and having a non-pointed top, shall be placed at each corner; a similar flag-post may be placed opposite the half-way line on each side of the field of play, not less than 1 yard outside the touch-line. A half-way line shall be marked out across the field of play. The centre of the field of play shall be indicated by a suitable mark and a circle with a 10 yards radius shall be marked round it.

(3) The Goal-Area. At each end of the field of play two lines shall be drawn at right-angles to the goal-line, 6 yards from each goal-post. These shall extend into the field of play for a distance of 6 yards and shall be joined by a line drawn parallel with the goal-line. Each of the spaces enclosed by these lines and the goal-line shall be called a goal-area.

(4) The Penalty-Area. At each end of the field of play two lines shall be drawn at right-angles to the goal-line, 18 yards from each goal-post. These shall extend into the field of play for a distance of 18 yards and shall be joined by a line drawn parallel with the goal-line. Each of the spaces enclosed by these lines and the goal-line shall be called a penalty-area. A suitable mark shall be made within each penalty-area, 12 yards from the mid-point of the goal-line, measured along an undrawn line at right-angles thereto. These shall be the penalty-kick marks. From each penalty-kick mark an arc of a circle, having a radius of 10 yards, shall be drawn outside the penalty-area.

(5) The Corner-Area. From each corner-flag post a quarter circle, having a radius of 1 yard, shall be drawn inside the field of play.

(6) The Goals. The goals shall be placed on the centre of each goal-line and shall consist of two upright posts, equidistant from the corner-flags and 8 yards apart (inside measurement), joined by a horizontal cross-bar the lower edge of which shall be 8 ft. from the ground. The width and depth of the cross-bars shall not exceed 5 inches (12 cm). The goal-posts and the cross-bars shall have the same width.

Nets may be attached to the posts, cross-bars and ground behind the goals. They should be appropriately supported and be so placed as to allow the goalkeeper ample room.

Footnote:
   Goal-nets. The use of nets made of

hemp, jute or nylon is permitted. The nylon strings may, however, not be thinner than those made of hemp or jute.

Decisions of The International F.A. Board

(1) In international matches the dimensions of the field of play shall be: maximum 110 × 75 metres; minimum 100 × 64 metres.

(2) National Associations must adhere strictly to these dimensions. Each National Association organising an international match must advise the visiting Association, before the match, of the place and the dimensions of the field of play.

(3) The Board has approved this table of measurements for the Laws of the Game:

130 yards	....	120 metres
120 yards	....	110
110 yards	....	100
100 yards	....	90
80 yards	....	75
70 yards	....	64
50 yards	....	45
18 yards	....	16.50
12 yards	....	11
10 yards	....	9.15
8 yards	....	7.32
6 yards	....	5.50
1 Yard	....	1
8 feet	....	2.44
5 feet	....	1.50
28 inches	....	0.71
27 inches	....	0.68
9 inches	....	0.22
5 inches	....	0.12
3/4 inch	....	0.019
1/2 inch	....	0.0127
3/8 inch	....	0.010
14 ounces	....	396 grams
16 ounces	....	453 grams

8.5 lb./sq.in.	....	600 gr/cm²
15.6 lb./sq.in.	....	1100 gr/cm²

(4) The goal-line shall be marked the same width as the depth of the goal-posts and the cross-bar, so that the goal-line and goal-posts will conform to the same interior and exterior edges.

(5) The 6 yards (for the outline of the goal-area) and the 18 yards (for the outline of the penalty-area) which have to be measured along the goal-line, must start from the inner sides of the goal-posts.

(6) The space within the inside areas of the field of play includes the width of the lines marking these areas.

(7) All Associations shall provide standard equipment, particularly in international matches, when the Laws of the Game must be complied with in every respect and especially with regard to the size of the ball and other equipment which must conform to the regulations. All cases of failure to provide standard equipment must be reported to FIFA.

(8) In a match played under the rules of a competition if the cross-bar becomes displaced or broken, play shall be stopped and the match abandoned unless the cross-bar has been repaired and replaced in position or a new one provided without such being a danger to the players. A rope is not considered to be a satisfactory substitute for a cross-bar.

In a friendly match, by mutual consent, play may be resumed without the cross-bar provided it has been removed and no longer constitutes a danger to the players. In these circumstances, a rope may be used as a substitute for a cross-bar. If a rope is not used and the ball crosses the goal-line at a point which, in the opinion of the referee is below where the cross-bar should have been, he shall award a goal.

The game shall be restarted by the referee dropping the ball at the place where it was when play was stopped, unless it was within the goal-area at that time, in which case it shall be dropped on that part of the goal-area line which runs parallel to the goal-line, at the point nearest to where the ball was when play was stopped.

(9) National Associations may specify such maximum and minimum dimensions for the cross-bars and goal-posts, within the limits laid down in Law I, as they consider appropriate.

(10) Goal-posts and cross-bars must be made of wood, metal or other approved material as decided from time to time by the International FA Board. They may be square, rectangular, round, half-round or elliptical in shape.

Goal-posts and cross-bars made of other materials and in other shapes are not permitted. The goal-posts must be of white colour.

(11) 'Curtain-raisers' to international matches should only be played following agreement on the day of the match, and taking into account the condition of the field of play, between representatives of the two Associations and the referee (of the international match).

(12) National Associations, particularly in international matches, should

− restrict the number of photographers around the field of play,
− have a line (photographers' line) marked behind the goal-lines at least two metres from the corner flag going through a point situated at least 3.5 metres behind the intersection of the goal-line with the line marking the goal-area to a point situated at least six metres behind the goal-posts,
− prohibit photographers from passing over these lines,
− forbid the use of artificial lighting in the form of "flashlights".

Law II – The Ball

The ball is the heart of the game, the "magic" spherical object which reveals the abilities of players by reproducing and measuring their skills. It is about the size of a man's head, made from "safe" materials, inflated to a pressure which allows for variations in altitude and methods of manufacture, and not too heavy to be dangerous.

Modern soccer balls are high technology products but selecting the match ball does not need to be a precise science. It should simply be suited to the conditions of play.

A hard ball is difficult to control on a hard surface because of excessive bounce causing errors of judgement, dangerous play, more ball-to-hand

A hard ball on a hard surface causes frustration and loss of enjoyment

contact, more out-of-play stoppages, all adding up to frustration and consequent loss of enjoyment. A soft ball on a wet or muddy surface becomes a dull object with uncertain bounce, little roll, less vitality, less interest, all affecting the potential for enjoying the game.

Referees can avoid these problems by testing the match ball on the field before the game – in good time to adjust the ball pressure if necessary. A sound general rule to follow is – hard ground/soft ball : soft ground/hard ball.

The ball may only be changed with the consent of the referee. In some countries one sees several reserve balls placed around the field with the object of replacing the match ball quickly should it leave the immediate area of the field. This is acceptable provided that the referee is satisfied that a replacement ball meets the requirements of the law.

The ball can burst or become deflated. Rare, but this phenomenon occurred in consecutive FA Cup Finals with the added curiosity that one club played in both matches. They were in 1946, Charlton Athletic v Derby County, and 1947, Charlton v Burnley.

Decisions 4 and 5 indicate how play is restarted after a ball becomes defective.

LAW II
The Ball

The ball shall be spherical; the outer casing shall be of leather or other approved materials. No material shall be used in its construction which might prove dangerous to the players.

The circumference of the ball shall not be more than 28 inches and not less than 27 inches. The weight of the ball at the start of the game shall not be more than 16 oz. nor less than 14 oz. The pressure shall be equal to 0.6–1.1 atmosphere (=600–1,100 gr/cm^2) at sea level. The ball shall not be changed during the game unless authorised by the referee.

Decisions of The International F.A. Board

(1) The ball used in any match shall be considered the property of the Association or Club on whose ground the match is played, and at the close of play it must be returned to the referee.

(2) The International Board, from time to time, shall decide what constitutes approved materials. Any approved material shall be certified as such by the International Board.

(3) The Board has approved these equivalents of the weights specified in the Law: 14 to 16 ounces – 396 to 453 grammes.

(4) If the ball bursts or becomes deflated during the course of a match, the game shall be stopped and restarted by dropping the new ball at the place where the first ball became defective, unless it was within the goal-area at that time, in which case it shall be dropped on that part of the goal-area line which runs parallel to the goal-line, at the point nearest to where the ball was when play was stopped

(5) If this happens during a stoppage of the game (place-kick, goal-kick, corner-kick, free-kick, penalty-kick or throw-in), the game shall be restarted accordingly.

Law III – Number of Players

Although early laws made no mention of the number of players it was the practice for heads of teams to agree to eleven-a-side games. The practice was first recognised in the rules of the FA Challenge Cup, founded in

1871, and later incorporated into the laws.

One player must be designated as a goalkeeper but his role is not defined. The original definition read, "a goalkeeper is the defender who, for the time being, is nearest to his own goal" and "shall be at liberty to use his hands for the protection of his goal". At that time all players were dressed alike so the goalkeeper was identified by personal characteristics, such as a beard, although some wore a cap which aided recognition. Nowadays, goalkeepers wear colours different from the other players.

The "liberty" of using hands was generous because it applied to the whole of the defending teams half of the field. In the laws of 1912 this privilege was reduced to the penalty-area and has remained so.

The role of the goalkeeper developed from the single task of preventing the ball from passing through the goal to that of a specialist with much influence on team tactics. In recent years the handling privilege became abused leading to unreasonable possession of the ball, delaying tactics and undue emphasis on negative defensive play. In Law XII we shall see how restrictions have been imposed on the goalkeeper with the intention of encouraging attacking play.

Interestingly, the law does not mention the actual positions of players. It is obvious that the goalkeeper will position himself near to his goal to take advantage of his handling privilege but he is not prevented from moving to any part of the field. Some modern goalkeepers create interest and excitement by leaving the penalty area for sorties towards the opponents goal. The Colombian goalkeeper, José René Higuita, demonstrated this during the 1990 World Cup matches in Italy.

Any player may change places with the goalkeeper during a normal stoppage in play and provided that the referee is notified.

As for the "outfield" players the law wisely says nothing, allowing complete freedom for team managers to devise tactics which combine individual skills in the best interest of team play.

About 95% of the text of this law deals with substitutions of any of the basic team of eleven allowing up to two in official competition matches and not more than five in other matches.

Substitutes were originally permitted when players were injured, in order to maintain numerical equality, but not in competition matches. There was a reluctance to allow substitutions in all matches because it was thought that the character of the game would suffer. Television had an influence on a change of view when millions of fans saw several

Eleven World Champions. The German team, winners of the 1990 World Cup.
Photo: Peter Robinson

Procedure for substitutions

important matches, such as FA Cup Finals, spoiled by the spectacle of injured players continuing under obvious stress.

The law does not restrict substitutions to injured players but the spirit behind this concession remains despite the frequent use of replacements for tactical reasons.

The procedure for a substitution is:

a. there is a normal stoppage in the game;
b. the referee is notified;
c. the outgoing player has left the field;
d. the referee signals permision for the new player to enter the field;
e. the new player enters at the half-way line.

Replaced players take no further part in the game. This prevents the re-use of a player considered to have been injured seriously enough to be substituted and restricts an extension of tactical substitutions.

The minimum number of players in a team may be fixed by National Associations although the International Board recommend a minimum of seven.

Players must obtain the permission of the referee to enter or leave the field. All substitutes are subject to the authority and jurisdiction of the referee whether called upon to play or not. They are members of the team and may be disciplined for any misconduct reported by the referee.

LAW III
Number of Players

(1) A match shall be played by two teams, each consisting of not more than eleven players, one of whom shall be the goalkeeper.

(2) Substitutes may be used in any match played under the rules of an official competition under the jurisdiction of FIFA, Conferences or National Associations, subject to the following conditions:

(a) that the authority of the international association(s) or National Association(s) concerned has been obtained.

(b) that, subject to the restriction contained in the following paragraph (c), the rules of a competition shall state how many, if any, substitutes may be nominated and how many of those nominated may be used.

(c) that a team shall not be permitted to use more than two substitutes in any match who must be chosen from not more than five players whose names may (subject to the rules of the competition) be required to be given to the referee prior to the commencement of the match.

(3) Substitutes may be used in any other match, provided that the two teams concerned reach agreement on a maximum number, not exceeding five, and that the terms of such agreement are intimated to the referee, before the match. If the referee is not informed, or if the teams fail to reach agreement, no more than two substitutes shall be permitted. In all cases the substitutes must be chosen from not more than five players whose names may be required to be given to the referee prior to the commencement of the match.

(4) Any of the other players may change places with the goalkeeper, provided that the referee is informed before the change is made, and provided also that the change is made during a stoppage of the game.

(5) When a goalkeeper or any other player is to be replaced by a substitute, the following conditions shall be observed:

(a) The referee shall be informed of the proposed substitution, before it is made.

(b) The substitute shall not enter the field of play until the player he is replacing has left, and then only after having received a signal from the referee.

(c) He shall enter the field during a stoppage in the game, and at the half-way line.

(d) A player who has been replaced shall not take any further part in the game.

(e) A substitute shall be subject to the authority and jurisdiction of the referee whether called upon to play or not.

(f) The substitution is completed when the substitute enters the field of play, from which moment he becomes a player and the player whom he is replacing ceases to be a player.

Punishment

(a) Play shall not be stopped for an infringement of paragraph 4. The players concerned shall be cautioned immediately the ball goes out of play.

(b) If a substitute enters the field of play without the authority of the referee, play shall be stopped. The substitute shall be cautioned and removed from the field or sent off according to the circumstances. The game shall be restarted by the referee dropping the ball at the place where it was when play was stopped, unless it was within the goal-area at that time, in which case it shall be dropped on that part of the goal-area line which runs parallel to the goal-line, at the point nearest to where the ball was when play was stopped.

(c) For any other infringement of this Law, the player concerned shall be cautioned, and if the game is stopped by the referee to administer the caution, it shall be restarted by an indirect free-kick, to be taken by a player of the opposing team from the place where the ball was when play was stopped subject to the overriding conditions imposed in Law XIII.

(d) If a competition's rules require the names of substitutes to be given to the referee prior to the commencement of the match, then failure to do so will mean that no substitutes can be permitted.

Decisions of The International F.A. Board

(1) The minimum number of players in a team is left to the discretion of National Associations.

(2) The Board is of the opinion that a match should not be considered valid if there are fewer than seven players in either of the teams.

(3) A player who has been ordered off before play begins may only be replaced by one of the named substitutes. The kick-off must not be delayed to allow the substitute to join

his team.

A player who has been ordered off after play has started may not be replaced.

A named substitute who has been ordered off, either before or after play has started, may not be replaced.

(This decision only relates to players who are ordered off under Law XII. It does not apply to players who have infringed Law IV.)

Law IV – Players' Equipment

Soccer is not a dangerous sport but there is a clear message in this law for safety and protection. The signficant word in the first sentence is "compulsory". It applies not only to an acceptable uniform but also to the responsibility of players to protect themselves from injury.

Most injuries in soccer affect the legs below the knees but, although shinguards have been worn since 1874 (invented by S. Widdowson) they were not made compulsory equipment until 1990.

Soccer boots, the most frequent cause of injury, were the subject of hundreds of words in this law before 1990. Detailed technical specifications, intended mainly for manufacturers and to guide referees, regulated the shapes, sizes, materials, and numbers of studs and bars. Now, soccer footwear is just one of the elements of the all-embracing directive that "A player shall not wear anything which is dangerous to another player."

This emphasises the responsibility of the player to choose footwear with great care and to ensure that the element of danger, inherent in studs and bars, is kept within reason. Hard surfaces will quickly wear studs to

Why shinguards are compulsory

Shin protection – ancient shinguards over bare legs

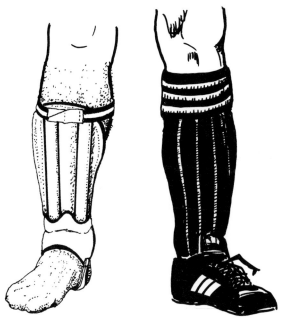

... and modern. Shinguards must be covered entirely by stockings

Steel toe-caps were needed in heavy boots to punt a heavy leather ball.
Today, lightweight shoes help players to caress the modern style ball with greater
accuracy and pace

sharp edges. Soft surfaces will tempt players to fit extra long studs.

Watches, rings, pendants, solid plaster casts, leg supports, and even some goalkeepers' gloves, are elements of danger which can be avoided.

Referees have a clear duty to inspect players' equipment before every match in good time to allow adjustments to be completed. To underline the point the whole world was kept waiting for the start of the 1978 World Cup Final, between Argentina and Holland, when the Dutch player Van de Kerkhof appeared on the field wearing a plaster cast on a hand. Argentine players protested to the referee who was obliged to allow several minutes for the cast to be covered. The incident created much bad feeling which could have been avoided.

LAW IV
Players' Equipment

(1) (a) The basic compulsory equipment of a player shall consist of a jersey or shirt, shorts, stockings, shinguards and footwear.

(b) A player shall not wear anything which is dangerous to another player.

(2) Shinguards, which must be covered entirely by the stockings, shall be made of a suitable material (rubber, plastic, polyurethane or similar substance) and shall afford a reasonable degree of protection.

(3) The goalkeeper shall wear colours which distinguish him from the other players and from the referee.

Punishment

For any infringement of this Law, the player at fault shall be instructed to leave the field of play by the referee, to adjust his equipment or obtain any missing equipment, when the ball next ceases to be in play, unless by then the player has already corrected his equipment. Play shall not be stopped immediately for an infringement of this Law. A player who is instructed to leave the field to adjust his equipment or obtain missing equipment shall not return without first reporting to the referee, who shall satisfy himself that the player's equipment is in order. The player shall only re-enter the game at a moment when the ball has ceased to be in play.

Decisions of the International F.A. Board

(1) In international matches, international competitions, international club competitions and friendly matches between clubs of different National Associations, the referee, prior to the start of the game, shall inspect the players' equipment and prevent any player whose equipment does not conform to the requirements of this Law from playing until such time as it does comply. The rules of any competition may include a similar provision.

(2) If the referee finds that a player is wearing articles not permitted by the Laws and which may constitute a danger to other players, he shall order him to take them off. If he fails to carry out the referee's instruction, the player shall not take part in the match.

(3) A player who has been prevented from taking part in the game or a player who has been sent off the field for infringing Law IV must report to the referee during a stoppage of the game and may not enter or re-enter the field of play unless and until the referee has satisfied himself that the player is no longer infringing Law IV.

(4) A player who has been prevented from taking part in a game or who has been sent off because of an infringement of Law IV, and who enters or re-enters the field of play to join or re-join his team, in breach of the conditions of Law XII, (j), shall be cautioned.

If the referee stops the game to administer the caution, the game shall be restarted by an indirect free-kick, taken by a player of the opposing side, from the place where the ball was when the referee stopped the game, subject to the overriding conditions imposed in Law XIII.

6
Control

Law V – **Referees**
Law VI – **Linesmen**

Referees and linesmen

Many soccer games are played without qualified referees and linesmen because there is a shortage of officials in relation to the demand. A game cannot be played to its full potential unless a neutral person is available to decide points of contention promptly and to guide the play within the framework of the laws. The match officials contribute much to the enjoyment of players and spectators by interfering as little as is necessary to maintain control and ensure that fair play is observed.

Laws V and VI describe the duties and responsibilities of match officials and the exceptional authority delegated to them by the administrators of the game.

The referee arrives in the nick of time. Photo: FIFA

Law V – Referees

Definition: "Referee: One to whom a matter in dispute is referred for decision."

Applied to the role of the soccer referee this definition was appropriate in the last century when the referee, a neutral person, waited on the touch-line for appeals for decisions from two umpires, appointed by the teams, standing in the field of play. His role was passive and remained so until 1891 when a mounting frequency of disputes caused many interruptions in play. To enforce the laws promptly and more efficiently the referee was transferred into the game while the umpires moved to the touch-lines to become linesmen.

The original function of the referee, "to decide disputed points", appeared in the laws until 1973 when it was finally recognised that his duties and responsibilities had evolved to cover all aspects of an organised game.

Today, the principal match official is, effectively, a superintendent of play. The definition:

"Superintendent: One who manages and directs; has charge and oversight of an activity; controls with authority."

is more appropriate and sums up the job specification of the referee detailed in Law V.

It amounts to total power to supervise, manage, direct and control the conduct of a soccer game.

Only referees know the enormous amount of time devoted to studying the meaning and practical interpretation of the fine print of every law. Every referee is required to be a trained expert, to attend regular courses, seminars, discussion groups, absorb advice from senior colleagues and apply this knowledge on the field by recognising instantly any infringement and then to impose the correct discipline with firmness and dignity.

From the foregoing summary it is clear that a dedicated referee is a person with a deep passion for the game, well trained in theory and practice and having the courage to make instant decisions, however, unpopular they may be. Add another essential requirement, a physical condition equivalent to an athlete, and we are describing a very special person in soccer, a person to be saluted for an exceptional contribution to the well-being of our favourite sport.

Advantage

Further proof of the extraordinary powers granted to the referee is that the "advantage clause" V(b), allows him to set aside the written law and apply a personal interpretation of fair play by not stopping play for an offence if, in his opinion it would give an advantage to the offending team.

An obvious example would be where an attacker is tripped but, before the referee stops play, he is able to continue with a good chance of scoring a goal. The referee allows play to proceed with a call of "advantage" and a signal to play on. Another example: a defender handles the ball just before it goes into the goal. Law XII requires a penalty-kick to be awarded but the offending team would benefit if the penalty-kick was not converted. The referee would allow the goal.

The referee will sometimes allow a free-kick to be taken quickly before opposing players have observed the 10 yards limit, required by Law XIII, considering that delay would be to the advantage of the offending team.

When should advantage be applied? So much depends on the attitude and sportsmanship of the players as to whether the game can be allowed to flow or require constant checking for rough or illegal play. Generally, referees are advised to exercise caution in the first few minutes in order to establish clear authority.

Advantage should always be allowed when a goal is almost certain but not in cases of serious misconduct or injury. Clear communication of advantage is important. Situations arise where an offence has been seen by the players and spectators but, in the opinion of the referee, play should continue. If the referee's thinking is not clearly understood it is often concluded that either the official missed the offence or considered that it was not an offence. The official may have made an excellent decision but poor communication invites criticism to the detriment of his authority and pleasure of the game.

Clear communication of referees' decisions is of concern to all. Not only should the players be aware of the reasons for stopping play but also, as the sport has such a wide spectator appeal, those who watch should be helped to understand the cause and effect of match incidents.

Studies have shown that referees want to communicate their decisions and do so by simple, instinctive gestures, e.g. touching an arm to indicate a handling offence, raising a foot to mime a dangerous kick, etc. The laws require only one signal from the referee – to raise one arm to signify that a free-kick is indirect (Law XIII – Decision 1). Other approved signals are illustrated on pages 77–85.

The referee is required to keep the game moving by interfering as little as possible, dealing firmly with clear breaches of the laws and stopping play for a seriously injured player to be removed for treatment. Other less serious injuries can be dealt with on the touch-line. In cases of doubt the referee may allow a team official (preferably a medical person) to enter the field and to examine the player but not to carry out treatment. In some countries the referee displays a green card to confirm that an official may enter the field.

Recent alarm over the transmission of serious diseases, via blood spilled at sports injuries, moved the International Board to issue a directive to referees to:

Advantage. A foul has been committed here but play is allowed to continue as there is a good chance of a goal being scored

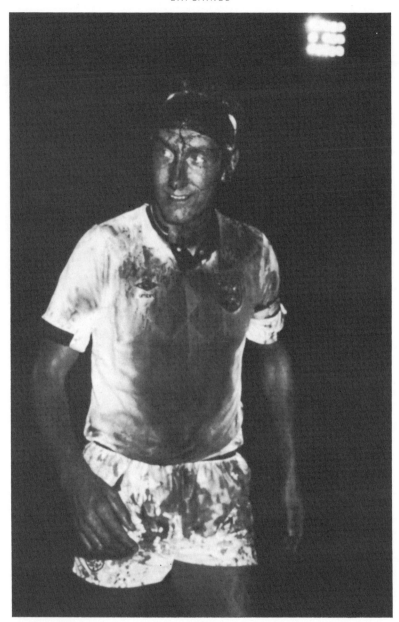

A sight which should never again be seen on a soccer field. Referees are directed to insist that badly injured players leave the field for adequate treatment. Photo: Bob Thomas "prevent any player, who is bleeding profusely, from taking any further part in a match until he has been adequately treated and the bleeding has stopped."

The referee has total command over who enters or leaves the field and to stop, suspend or abandon a game where the elements, interference by spectators, or any other cause, makes such action necessary. Apart from the formal duties and responsibilities prescribed for controlling on-the-field action the modern referee must be concerned with supervising off-the-field coaching. Since 1993 team coaches have had the right to convey tactical instructions to players during a match. This was a major departure from the fundamental principle, held sacred for 130 years, that players be allowed freedom to solve problems in their own way.

Rigid and aggressive coaching stifles spontaneity, causes irritation, frustration and incitement to misconduct. It also affects the dignity of the game.

The referee is therefore concerned to ensure that coaching is contained within reasonable bounds.

Where large audiences may be present at a match the referee is required to consider the welfare of all concerned by consulting with security authorities and those in charge of law and order.

Referees who have charge of matches at national and international levels have travelled a long road, serving an apprenticeship for several years in junior and senior amateur soccer. They are all human and can make errors but, as a neutral official, the referee's decision must always be accepted as final even when it may be seen to be wrong. Self-discipline is, after all, one of the qualities of character fundamental to the well-being of the individual and the sport.

Rigid and aggressive coaching during play can stifle spontaneity, cause irritation and frustration for players

LAW V
Referees

A referee shall be appointed to officiate in each game. His authority and the exercise of the powers granted to him by the Laws of the Game commence as soon as he enters the field of play.

His power to penalise shall extend to offences committed when play has been temporarily suspended, or when the ball is out of play. His decision on points of fact connected with the play shall be final, so far as the result of the game is concerned. He shall:

(a) enforce the laws.

(b) refrain from penalising in cases where he is satisfied that, by doing so, he would be giving an advantage to the offending team.

(c) keep a record of the game; act as timekeeper and allow the full or agreed time, adding thereto all time lost through accident or other cause.

(d) have discretionary power to stop the game for any infringement of the Laws and to suspend or terminate the game whenever, by reason of the elements, interference by spectators, or other cause, he deems such stoppage necessary. In such a case he shall submit a detailed report to the competent authority, within the stipulated time, and in accordance with the provisions set up by the National Association under whose jurisdiction the match was played. Reports will be deemed to be made when received in the ordinary course of post.

(e) from the time he enters the field of play, caution and show a yellow card to any player guilty of misconduct or ungentlemanly behaviour. In such cases the referee shall send the name of the offender to the competent authority, within the stipulated time, and in accordance with the provisions set up by the National Association under whose jurisdiction the match was played.

(f) allow no person other

than the players and linesmen to enter the field of play without his permission.

(g) stop the game if, in his opinion, a player has been seriously injured; have the player removed as soon as possible from the field of play, and immediately resume the game. If a player is slightly injured, the game shall not be stopped until the ball has ceased to be in play. A player who is able to go to the touch-line or goal-line for attention of any kind, shall not be treated on the field of play.

(h) send off the field of play and show a red card to any player who, in his opinion, is guilty of violent conduct, serious foul play, the use of foul or abusive language or who persists in misconduct after having received a caution.

(i) signal for recommencement of the game after all stoppages.

(j) decide that the ball provided for a match meets with the requirements of Law II.

Decisions of The International F.A. Board

(1) Referees in international matches shall wear a blazer or blouse the colour of which is distinct from the colours worn by the contesting teams.

(2) Referees for international matches will be selected from a neutral country unless the countries concerned agree to appoint their own officials.

(3) The referee must be chosen from the official list of international referees. This need not apply to amateur and youth international matches.

(4) The referee shall report to the appropriate authority misconduct or any misdemeanour on the part of spectators, officials, players, named substitutes or other persons which take place either on the field of play or in its vicinity at any time prior to, during, or after the match in question so that appropriate action can be taken by the authority concerned.

(5) Linesmen are assistants of the referee. In no case shall the referee consider the intervention of a linesman if he himself has seen the incident and from his position on the field, is better able to judge. With this reserve, and the linesman neutral, the referee can consider the intervention, and if the information of the linesman applies to that phase of the game immediately before the scoring of a goal, the referee may act thereon and

cancel the goal.

(6) The referee, however, can only reverse his first decision so long as the game has not been restarted.

(7) If the referee has decided to apply the advantage clause and to let the game proceed, he cannot revoke his decision if the presumed advantage has not been realised, even though he has not, by any gesture, indicated his decision. This does not exempt the offending player from being dealt with by the referee.

(8) The Laws of the Game are intended to provide that games should be played with as little interference as possible, and in this view it is the duty of referees to penalise only deliberate breaches of the Law. Constant whistling for trifling and doubtful breaches produces bad feeling and loss of temper on the part of the players and spoils the pleasure of spectators.

(9) By para. (d) of Law V the referee is empowered to terminate a match in the event of grave disorder, but he has no power or right to decide, in such event, that either team is disqualified and thereby the loser of the match. He must send a detailed report to the proper authority who alone has power to deal further with this matter.

(10) If a player commits two infringements of a different nature at the same time, the referee shall punish the more serious offence.

(11) It is the duty of the referee to act upon the information of neutral linesmen with regard to incidents that do not come under the personal notice of the referee.

(12) The referee shall not allow any person to enter the field of play until play has stopped, and only then if he has given him a signal to do so.

(13) The coach may convey tactical instructions to players during the match.

The coach and other officials, however, must remain within the confines of the technical area,* where such an area is provided and they must conduct themselves, at all times, in a responsible manner.

(14) In tournaments or competitions where a fourth official is appointed, his role and duties shall be in accordance with the guide-lines approved by the International Football Association Board.

* In the higher echelons of the game, where such a technical area is defined, the latter may be defined suitably in terms of **the length of the bench plus one meter at each side of the bench, and the area in front of the bench up to one meter parallel to the touch-line.**

Signals by The Referee and Linesmen

The signals illustrated in this memorandum have been approved by the International F.A. Board for use by registered referees of affiliated National Associations.

Illustrations concerning signals by the referee are shown on pages 77–85. They are simple, universally in use, and well understood.

While it is not the duty of the referee to explain or mime any offence that has caused him to give a particular decision, there are times when a simple gesture or word of guidance can aid communication and assist toward greater understanding, and gaining more respect, to the mutual benefit of referee and players. Improving communication should be encouraged, but the exaggerated miming of offences can be undignified and confusing and should not be used.

An indication by the referee of the point where a throw-in should be taken may well help prevent a player from taking a throw-in improperly. A call of "Play on, advantage" confirms to a player that the referee has not simply missed a foul, but has chosen to apply advantage. Even an indication that the ball was minutely deflected by its touching another player on its path across a touch-line might be helpful too in generating a greater understanding between referee and players. A better understanding will lead to more harmonious relationships.

All signals given by the referee should be simple, clear and instinctive. They should be designed to control the game efficiently and to ensure continuous play as far as possible; they are intended essentially to indicate what the next action in the game should be, not principally to justify that action.

An arm pointing to indicate a corner-kick, goal-kick or foul, and the direction in which it is to be taken, will normally be sufficient. The raised arm to indicate that a free-kick is indirect is clearly understood, but if a player queries politely whether the award is a direct free-kick or an indirect free-kick, a helpful word from the referee, in addition to the regular signal, will lead to a better understanding in future.

The proper use of the whistle, voice and hand signals by the referee and the flags by the linesmen should all assist understanding through clear communication.

Direct free-kick
The hand and arm clearly indicate the direction

Indirect free-kick
This signal shall be maintained until the kick has been taken and retained until the ball
has been played or touched by another player or goes out of play.

Play on – advantage
Where the referee sees an offence but uses the "advantage", he shall indicate that play shall continue.

Goal-kick

Goal-kick

Corner-kick

Caution or expulsion
With the card system, the card shall be shown in the manner illustrated. The player's
identity must be recorded at the time.

Penalty-kick
The referee clearly indicates the penalty-spot, but there is no need
to run towards it.

Law VI – Linesmen

Referees are instructed to use linesmen as assistant referees because neutral linesmen are qualified referees in their own right and are controlling matches in the middle when not doing duty as linesmen. Effectively, three qualified officials supervise the play.

In addition to the obvious assistance of signalling the ball out of play, which side is entitled to restart the game and when a substitution is required, (as shown on pages 88–97), neutral linesmen assist the referee before the game starts with inspections of the field and equipment. They keep a check on timing of play, are expected to call the attention of the referee to rough play or ungentlemanly conduct, give an opinion on any point put to them by the referee and generally assist in conducting the game in accordance with the laws.

Linesmen's signals are essentially for the information of the referee. Players should not stop when a linesman's flag is raised but play to the referee's whistle. The referee may have seen the incident from a better angle or may decide to use advantage.

When neutral officials are not available each team is expected to appoint a club official to act as linesman. Their duties are usually restricted to signalling when the ball crosses a boundary line and indicating which team should restart play. However, other duties may be delegated by the referee but he has the ultimate responsibility for all decisions.

It is a fact that not all good referees make good linesmen. Studies of World Cup tournaments have shown up serious deficiencies among top referees when given a linesman's role. FIFA decided in 1990 to create a special panel of linesmen for international matches.

LAW VI
Linesmen

Two linesmen shall be appointed, whose duty (subject to the decision of the referee) shall be to indicate:

(a) when the ball is out of play,

(b) which side is entitled to a corner-kick, goal-kick or

throw-in,

(c) when a substitution is desired.

They shall also assist the referee to control the game in accordance with the Laws. In the event of undue interference or improper conduct by a linesman, the referee shall dispense with his services and arrange for a substitute to be appointed. (The matter shall be reported by the referee to the competent authority.) The linesmen should be equipped with flags by the club on whose ground the match is played.

Decisions of the International F.A. Board

(1) Linesmen, where neutral, shall draw the referee's attention to any breach of the Laws of the Game of which they become aware if they consider that the referee may not have seen it, but the referee shall always be the judge of the decision to be taken.

(2) National Associations are advised to appoint official referees of neutral nationality to act as linesmen in international matches.

(3) In international matches linesmen's flags shall be of a vivid colour, bright reds and yellows. Such flags are recommended for use in all other matches.

(4) A linesman may be subject to disciplinary action only upon a report of the referee for unjustified interference or insufficient assistance.

Off-side
Flag held upright to indicate off-side.

Off-side
When the referee stops play, linesman indicates position on far side of the field

Off-side
Position near the centre of the field.

Off-side
Position on near side of the field.

Substitution
Front view of the linesman signalling to the referee when a substitute is waiting on the touch-line.

Throw-in

Goal-kick

Corner-kick

The linesman may first need to signal that the ball has gone out of play if there is any doubt. He should also look at the referee in case he has already made his own decision which may be different from the linesman's.

7
Game Rules

Law VII – **Duration of the Game**
Law VIII – **The Start of Play**
Law IX   – **Ball in and out of Play**
Law X   – **Method of Scoring**

Basic procedures

As in any other sport this group of laws outlines basic procedure for the duration of play, how to start a game, when the ball is in or out of play and method of scoring.

Law VII – Duration of the Game

The normal duration of a game has stood the test of time since the mid-1880s. Divided into two 45 minute periods, with a compulsory break at half-time, players have a reasonable time to demonstrate individual and team skills without exhaustion.

There are exceptions. Teams may agree to play a friendly match to last as long as they wish and a shorter duration is allowed for under-16-year-olds, veteran and women players. Some competitions may have a special rule requiring teams to play extra-time, usually two periods of 15 minutes, to try and achieve a definite result.

The actual time that the ball is in play varies from game to game. A study of the 52 matches played in Italy during the 1990 World Cup produced an average of less than 60 minutes with the longest timed at 67 minutes and the shortest at 50 minutes. The study makes the point that each game has its own character. One match may flow fairly easily whereas another may require many stoppages. In Italy the stoppages ranged from a minimum of 86 to a maximum of 144!

For many years it has been common practice for the referee to make no allowance for time taken up during routine stoppages, e.g. when the ball goes out of play over the touch or goal-lines. However, recent trends in the game have led to an unacceptable loss of ball-in-play time. Deliberate time-wasting tactics, more frequent use of substitutions and greater concern for injured players have persuaded the International Board to tighten up this law and to instruct referees to be more strict in making due allowances.

Every player has the right to an interval at half-time and while the law says that this should not exceed 5 minutes modern practice stretches this to up to 15 minutes because the game has become faster and more physically demanding. However, where players are exposed to extreme climatic conditions the 5-minute interval should be respected.

How much time to allow is always at the discretion of the referee. He is the only recognised timekeeper and makes his judgements according to the circumstances in each game.

The referee has no option but to extend time to allow a penalty-kick to be completed if awarded at the end of the first or second periods. This was written into the law after an incident in a match played between Stoke City and Aston Villa in 1892. Stoke were awarded a penalty with just two minutes left for play. The Aston Villa goalkeeper kicked the ball far out of the playing area and it could not be found within the time remaining. The referee was obliged to end the game. Stoke lost 1–0 and the law was amended to correct what was clearly seen to be a situation against the spirit of fair play.

An uncompleted match must be replayed unless the rules of the competition concerned allow the result to stand or award the match to one of the teams.

The latter option was applied after an important World Cup qualifying match between Brazil and Chile played in Rio de Janeiro in 1989. After 69 minutes Brazil were leading 1–0 when the Chilean goalkeeper appeared to have been injured by a flare thrown onto the field by a fan. His injury seemed serious enough to the Chilean players to justify refusing to continue the match and to claim a replay on neutral territory.

FIFA's subsequent enquiry proved that the goalkeeper had not been injured but had taken part in an attempt to have the match abandoned. The match was awarded to Brazil, as a 2–0 victory. The goalkeeper, and several team officials, were severely punished for bringing the game into disrepute.

LAW VII
Duration of the Game

The duration of the game shall be two equal periods of 45 minutes, unless otherwise mutually agreed upon, subject to the following:

(a) Allowance shall be made in either period for all time lost through substition, the transport from the field of injured players, time-wasting or other cause, the amount of which shall be a matter for the discretion of the referee.

(b) Time shall be extended to permit a penalty-kick being taken at or after the expiration of the normal period in either half.

At half-time the interval shall not exceed 5 minutes except by consent of the referee.

Decisions of the International F.A. Board

(1) If a match has been stopped by the referee, before the completion of the time specified in the rules, for any reason stated in Law V, it must be re-played in full unless the rules of the competition concerned provide for the result of the match at the time of such stoppage to stand.

(2) Players have a right to an interval at half-time.

Law VIII – The Start of Play

The ceremony which takes place before a game starts can have an important influence on the result. After the referee has greeted the two captains a toss of a coin gives the winning captain a choice, first possession of the ball or the goal to defend (or to attack would be a more

The kick-off: opponents at least 10 yards from the ball. The ball must be kicked forward

positive approach).

Is there any difference? An astute captain will have already decided which option offers the best advantage for his team. He will have assessed the playing conditions, noting the immediate and possible influence of the sun, wind direction and strength, a sloping surface, etc. to decide whether choice of ends is preferable to first possession. A "lucky" end or the end where his team's supporters are gathered may be factors in his decision.

If there are no obvious advantages in direction of play first possession could offer the chance of a quick goal. There are many examples of goals scored within a few seconds of the kick-off to make this choice a match winner. Barrie Jones is recorded as having scored only 6 seconds after the kick-off for Notts County in a Football League match played in 1962, an extraordinary feat because a goal cannot be scored direct from the kick-off. The ball must be kicked forward and travel just over 2 feet before it is in play while opponents remain at least 10 yards away. The ball must be touched by a player other than the kicker and travel at least 50 yards (the minimum length of half the field) before passing the goalkeeper and entering the goal.

The team conceding the goal is given possession of the ball for a place-kick (kick-off). An interesting early rule of Harrow School required teams to change ends after a goal was scored, or, "if no goal has been obtained by 3 o'clock" – an example of equalising playing conditions!

The team which does not have first possession at the start of play restarts with a place-kick after the half-time interval.

There are rare occasions when a game is started by the referee dropping the ball between opposing players. This can occur anywhere on the field after the game has been stopped for a special reason, e.g. a serious injury or interference by an outside agency.

If extra periods of play are required the toss-up ceremony is repeated to decide choice of ends or kick-off.

Soccer law has such authority that a King, President, or any other person, is not allowed to start a match (IB Decision 2). The play must be decided by the players. A VIP is the equivalent of an illegal outside agency.

If a special ceremony is arranged, for a charity or exhibition match, the ball may be kicked but it must be returned to the centre-spot for a kick-off prescribed in this law.

LAW VIII
The Start of Play

(a) **At the beginning of the game,** choice of ends and the kick-off shall be decided by the toss of a coin. The team winning the toss shall have the option of choice of ends or the kick-off. The referee having given a signal, the game shall be started by a player taking a place-kick (i.e. a kick at the ball while it is stationary on the ground in the centre of the field of play) into his opponents' half of the field of play. Every player shall be in his own half of the field and every player of the team opposing that of the kicker shall remain not less than 10 yards from the ball until it is kicked-off; it shall not be deemed in play until it has travelled the distance of its own circumference. The kicker shall not play the ball a second time until it has been touched or played by another player.

(b) **After a goal has been scored**, the game shall be restarted in like manner by a player of the team losing the goal.

(c) **After half-time;** when re-starting after half-time, ends shall be changed and the kick-off shall be taken by a player of the opposite team to that of the player who started the game.

Punishment

For any infringement of this Law, the kick-off shall be re-taken, except in the case of the kicker playing the ball again before it has been touched or played by another player; for this offence an in-direct free-kick shall be taken by a player of the opposing team from the place where the infringement occurred, subject to the overriding con-ditions imposed in Law XIII.

A goal shall not be scored direct from a kick-off.

(d) **After any other tempo-rary suspension;** when re-starting the game after a temporary suspension of play from any cause not men-tioned elsewhere in these Laws, provided that immedi-ately prior to the suspension the ball has not passed over the touch- or goal-lines, the referee shall drop the ball at the place where it was when play was suspended, unless it was within the goal-area at that time, in which case it shall be dropped on that part of the goal-area line which runs parallel to the goal-line, at the point nearest to where the ball was when play was stopped. It shall be deemed in play when it has touched the ground; if, however, it goes over the touch- or goal-lines after it has been dropped by the referee, but before it is touched by a player, the refer-ee shall again drop it. A player shall not play the ball until it has touched the ground. If this section of the Laws is not complied with, the referee shall again drop the ball.

Decisions of the International F.A. Board

(1) If, when the referee drops the ball, a player infringes any of the Laws before the ball has touched the ground, the player concerned shall be cautioned or sent off the field according to the seriousness of the offence, but a free-kick cannot be awarded to the opposing team because the ball was not in play at the time of the offence. The ball shall therefore be again dropped by the referee.

(2) Kicking-off by persons other than the players competing in a match is prohibited.

Law IX – Ball in and out of Play

From the kick-off the ball is in play at all times until it crosses a boundary line or play is stopped by the referee.

The ball must "wholly cross' the boundary line. Whenever there is doubt, either for the ball being in or out of play, or, a possible infringement, the best advice for players is to, "Play to the whistle".

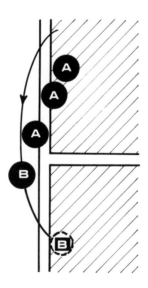

A's are IN PLAY
B's are OUT OF PLAY

LAW IX
Ball in and out of Play

The ball is out of play:

(a) when it has wholly crossed the goal-line or touch-line, whether on the ground or in the air.

(b) when the game has been stopped by the Referee.

The ball is in play at all other times from the start of the match to the finish including:

(a) if it rebounds from a goal-post, cross-bar or corner-flag post into the field of play.

(b) if it rebounds off either the referee or linesmen when they are in the field of play.

(c) in the event of a supposed infringement of the laws, until a decision is given.

Decisions of the International F.A. Board

(1) The lines belong to the areas of which they are the boundaries. In consequence, the touch-lines and the goal-lines belong to the field of play.

Law X – Method of Scoring

The main object of the game is to put the ball through the opponents goal in a legal manner. Normally, goals are scored with a foot or the head but any part of the body may be used except an arm or a hand. It would be legal if a goalkeeper threw the ball from his own penalty-area into the opponents goal but the possibility is so rare as to be practically non-existent. There are, however, cases of goalkeepers kicking the ball into the other goal after handling it inside their own penalty-area. Pat Jennings, goalkeeper for Tottenham Hotspur, accomplished this feat during the 1967 F.A. Charity Shield match against Manchester United.

A goal may not be scored if the ball is carried through the goal by an

NO

A goal is not scored until the ball has completely crossed the goal-line between the posts.
Credit: Pro Sport

NO

YES

opponent. Today, this would be a clear offence of hand ball but the word "carried" is significant because it was included in the original laws of 1863 to make the distinction between the soccer and rugby methods of play.

On the same principle as Law IX the whole of the ball must pass through the goal which means clearing the exterior edges of the goal-posts because, in Law I, the goal-lines and goal-posts must be of the same width.

If the ball wholly crosses the goal-line between the posts but spins or rebounds into play a goal is scored. This can be difficult to judge with a fast moving ball and requires excellent positioning by the match officials. A goal which caused much controversy was England's third against West Germany in the 1966 World Cup Final. From Geoff Hurst's shot the ball struck the underside of the cross-bar, dropped on or near the goal-line and rebounded into play to be headed away by a defender.

England players claimed a goal but the Germans insisted that the ball had not crossed the goal-line.

Was it a goal or not? Millions were kept waiting for the answer while the Swiss referee ran to the touch-line to consult the Russian linesman. Although not ideally placed the linesman pointed to the centre of the field to signal a goal.

Photographs and films have not satisfactorily proved the validity of the goal but history records that it was a vital factor in the result of the match won by England 4–2.

Defenders make mistakes and sometimes score against their own team – an "own goal". Bert Turner had this misfortune playing for Charlton against Derby County during the 1946 FA Cup Final but, one minute later, he scored again, this time in the opponents' goal!

Referees have been known to "score" goals when the ball has been deflected from them into the goal. Such a goal is valid because the referee is a neutral agent, equivalent to a moving goal-post.

A goal cannot be scored from a Place-kick (Law VIII), Indirect free-kick (Law XIII), Throw-in (Law XV), Goal-kick (Law XVI), or from a free-kick awarded to the defending team. Nor can a goal be allowed if interference occurs from an outside agent such as a spectator, animal or an object.

Nowadays, each goal is recorded by the referee in a notebook but an ancient practice was to "score" a notch in a goal-post! Effectively, players win goals but it is the referee who scores them!

England's controversial third goal against West Germany in the 1966 World Cup Final at Wembley. Did the whole of the ball cross the line? Photo: The Football Association

LAW X
Method of Scoring

Except as otherwise provided by these laws, a goal is scored when the whole of the ball has passed over the goal-line, between the goal-posts and under the cross-bar, provided it has not been thrown, carried or intentionally propelled by hand or arm, by a player of the attacking side, except in the case of a goalkeeper, who is within his own penalty-area.

The team scoring the greater number of goals during a game shall be the winner; if no goals or an equal number of goals are scored, the game shall be termed a "draw".

Decisions of the International F.A. Board

(1) Law X defines the only method according to which a match is won or drawn; no variation whatsoever can be authorised.

(2) A goal cannot in any case be allowed if the ball has been prevented by some outside agent from passing over the goal-line. If this happens in the normal course of play, other than at the taking of a penalty-kick, the game must be stopped and restarted by the referee dropping the ball at the place where the ball came into contact with the interference, unless it was within the goal-area at that time, in which case it shall be dropped on that part of the goal-area line which runs parallel to the goal-line, at the point nearest to where the ball was when play was stopped.

(3) If, when the ball is going into goal, a spectator enters the field before it passes wholly over the goal-line and tries to prevent a score, a goal shall be allowed if the ball goes into goal unless the spectator has made contact with the ball or has interfered with play, in which case the referee shall stop the game and restart it by dropping the ball at the place where the contact or interference occurred, unless it was within the goal-area at that time, in which case it shall be dropped on that part of the goal-area line which runs parallel to the goal-line, at the point nearest to where the ball was when play was stopped.

8
Technical

The off-side law is a technical law because it relates to tactical play while the ball is in motion. As will be seen from the extensive commentary on this law there is a sound reason for an off-side rule in soccer and other team games. It involves fair play, discipline, tactical innovation, skill and enjoyment.

When the basic elements are understood it is not difficult to follow how the law applies in practice. Players can improve their own and team performances when they know how to avoid off-side.

Law XI – Off-side

Off-side is the least understood and the most controversial law in soccer. It need not be as the following comments will attempt to explain.

The number of off-sides in a match can vary from zero (Italy v Poland 1982 World Cup) to as many as 22 (England v Kuwait '82 WC). The average in the 1990 World Cup was 8.32.

Why is off-side necessary in soccer? A tactical law, it is concerned with the position of players when the ball is in play. Its purpose is evident from a brief look at its origin and development.

Off-side can be related to the game of "harpastum", a form of mock battle played by Roman soldiers nearly 2000 years ago as part of military training exercises. Equal forces were assembled to contest the game on a limited area. The object was to capture an enemy stronghold by moving a ball, about the size of a man's head, to and behind the opponents' base line. In so doing the soldiers were taught how to combine as a unit to penetrate the opponents' defence using physical strength and intelligence in devising tactics to out-manoeuvre the opposition.

The game was taken up by Britons after the Roman garrisons were withdrawn. It retained the military objective but was contested between villages and towns. This led to the mob-football described earlier.

Around the 16th century the game became established in schools but, to maintain order and discipline, codes of conduct were drawn up to regulate play. A common feature of these early school games was emphasis on combined effort and team play with players moving as a unit behind the ball towards the defined target.

Any player caught in advance of the ball was considered to be out-of-play, off-the-side, off-side. In military terms he was out of the battle, out of his unit, off-the-strength.

In the sporting context to be off-side was unfair as indicated in the rules of school games in the last century:

No player is allowed to loiter between the ball and the adversaries' goal. (Cambridge Rules, 1856)

A player is "out-of-play" immediately he is in front of the ball and must return behind the ball as soon as possible. (Uppingham School, 1860)

A player is considered to be "sneaking" when only three or less opponents are before him and the opponents behind him. In such case he may not kick the ball. (Eton College, 1862)

The detail of early off-side rules stresses the same point, that the player had no right to interfere with play or an opponent. This restriction has influenced tactics of defence in moving forward to leave an opponent in limbo, the so called "off-side trap", accepted as a legitimate game strategy. Attackers must be alert to avoid being caught "behind enemy lines".

To underline the point that off-side is unfair play we know from our own experience as children that the player we despised the most was the one who placed himself close to goal waiting to score. The "goal-poacher", "goal-hanger", made little effort to help the other players, seeking the glory of scoring with the minimum of skill. At 6 or 7 years we did not understand the formal off-side law but inner feelings told us that this was not playing the game as it should be played.

Other team sports, rugby, hockey, even water polo, include an off-side rule on the same principle that attacking moves should develop as a combined team effort rather than rely on individual opportunism. The rule demands alertness and intelligence both on the part of attackers and defenders to constantly assess tactical movements and devise counter measures. It contributes much to the attractive fluidity and interest of the play.

Players who know the off-side law can improve performance to the benefit of the team. As an example, in an important international match, a famous England player destroyed eight potential goal-scoring moves by being caught off-side. One or two are excusable but not eight. The player did not understand the law or how to avoid off-side situations. In another match, previously mentioned, English players were ruled off-side on twenty of the twenty-two occasions recorded. The result was close, England won 1–0.

How does the off-side law work?

Every off-side situation involves just two basic elements:
1. Fact: the actual *position* of a player at *the moment the ball is played* by a team-mate, and
2. Opinion: whether he is *interfering* with play, or an opponent, or trying to gain an *unfair advantage*.

If a player is in advance of the ball, is not level with or does not have two or more opponents between himself and the goal-line, he is in an off-side position. This is a fact. To avoid being judged off-side the player must either return behind the ball, before it is played in his direction by a team-mate, or keep well clear of play and opponents involved in the play, because the referee has to form an opinion as to why he is in that position and his influence on the play.

If the England player had understood these simple elements he could have taken action to evade at least four off-side decisions. One of these occasions could have enabled an attack to result in the winning goal.

Why should off-side cause so much controversy? Basically, the problem is related to timing and difference of opinion.

Judgement of off-side position starts at the moment the ball is played. The referee and linesman must freeze in their minds the actual positions of attacking and defending players. This is rarely taken into account by players and spectators because of the natural tendency to follow the movement of the ball. The referee does not always stop play immediately because if the ball is kicked a long distance forward he needs time to judge whether the player, in an off-side position, is seeking to gain an advantage or will be close enough, when the ball arrives, to influence the next phase of play.

Each situation is seldom black or white. A player in an off-side position near the left touch-line will not be penalised if the ball is passed towards an on-side player near the right touch-line. He is too far away to interfere with the play.

In a similar incident but where the first player is near the centre of the field – a grey area – the referee must assess the player's actions and intentions before making a decision. In the meantime players' positions can change during the time taken for the ball to arrive in the next area of play. A perfectly correct off-side decision can appear unjust if the penalised player receives the ball in an on-side position. Conversely, a player may appear to be off-side but is not penalised because he has moved forward, from an on-side position, after the ball was kicked by a team-mate.

To assist referees, in judging interference and intention to gain advantage, the International Board stated, in 1924:

If a player in an off-side position advances towards an opponent or the ball and, in so doing, causes the play to be affected he should be penalised.

Judging off-side situations requires intense concentration by referees and linesmen, particularly when players' positions change rapidly. Because split-second decisions must be formed on the factors described a match official may err occasionally but not as often as it may seem from the point of view of the player or spectator.

A player is not penalised for off-side if he receives the ball direct from a goal-kick, a corner-kick or from a throw-in.

Summarising, the off-side law is a basic element of a team game where an objective is to be achieved through the combined skills of a group of players. It contributes to the fluidity of play, and tests alertness, intelligence and tactical innovation.

Off-side can be avoided if players remember three simple rules:

1. remain behind the ball, or,
2. keep at least two opponents between yourself and the goal-line; or,
3. keep clear of the next phase of play if in an off-side position.

Off-side judgements start at the moment the ball is played. Match officials concentrate on this factor while others tend to follow the ball. Interfering or attempting to gain an advantage are matters of opinion based on the actions and intentions of players in an off-side position.

Figure 6.2 shows several examples of off-side situations based on the positions of players when the ball is played.

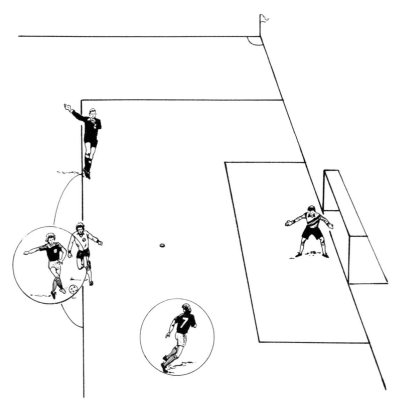

At the moment the ball is played number 7 is IN AN OFF-SIDE POSITION (not having at least two opponents between himself and the goal line.) He is clearly taking advantage (OPINION). Decision: OFF-SIDE

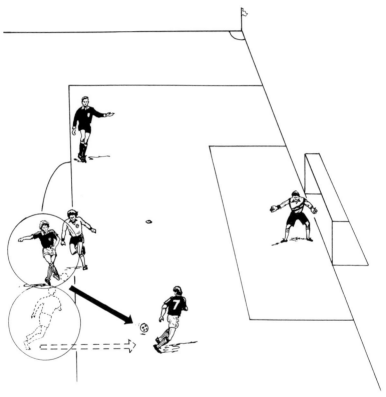

At the moment the ball is played number 7 is NOT IN AN OFF-SIDE POSITION (having at least two opponents between himself and the goal line.) Decision: NOT OFF-SIDE

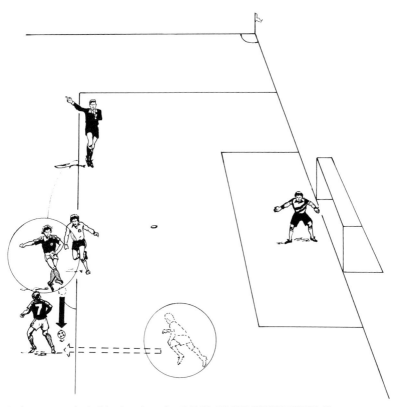

At the moment the ball is played number 7 IS IN AN OFF-SIDE POSITION. He cannot change this fact by running back to receive the ball in an on-side position. Decision: OFF-SIDE

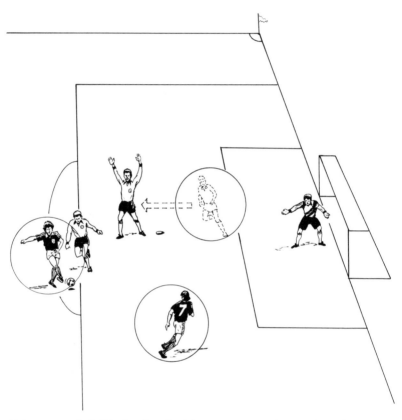

At the moment the ball is played number 7 has two opponents between himself and the goal-line. He is therefore NOT IN AN OFF-SIDE POSITION. The opponent cannot change this fact by running forward. DECISION: NOT OFF-SIDE

At the moment the ball is played number 11 IS IN AN OFF-SIDE POSITION (FACT) but is
NOT INTERFERING WITH PLAY (OPINION). Decision: NOT OFF-SIDE

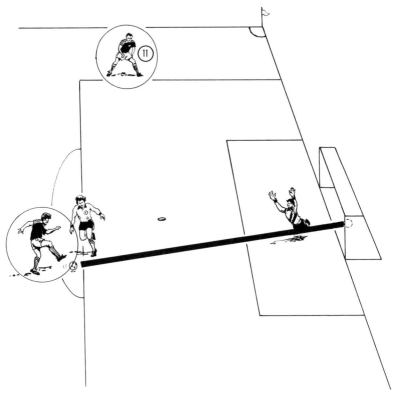

At the moment the ball is played number 11 IS IN AN OFF-SIDE POSITION but is NOT INTERFERING with play when the ball is kicked directly into the goal. Decision: A GOAL

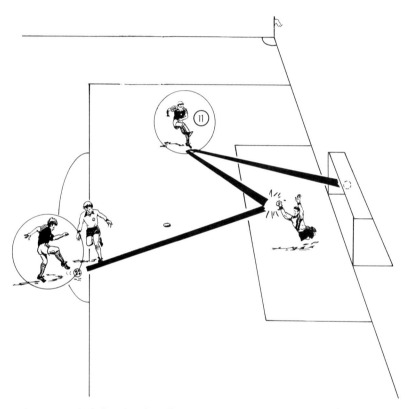

At the moment the ball is played number 11 IS IN AN OFF-SIDE POSITION. The ball is played by an opponent (goalkeeper) and he scores. The goal should be disallowed for OFF-SIDE if the referee considers that number 11 is interfering with play or gaining an advantage (OPINION)

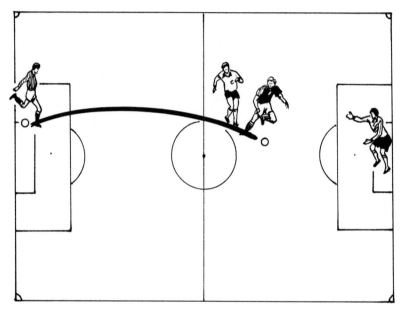

A player is NOT OFF-SIDE if the ball is received direct from a goal-kick

A player is NOT OFF-SIDE if the ball is received direct from a corner-kick

A player is NOT OFF-SIDE if the ball is received direct from a throw-in

LAW XI
Off-side

1. A player is in an off-side position if he is nearer to his opponents' goal-line than the ball, unless:

(a) he is in his own half of the field of play; or

(b) he is not nearer to his opponents' goal-line than at least two of his opponents.

2. A player shall only be declared off-side and penalised for being in an off-side position, if, at the moment the ball touches, or is played by, one of his team, he is, in the opinion of the referee

(a) interfering with play or with an opponent, or

(b) seeking to gain an advantage by being in that position.

3. A player shall not be declared off-side by the referee

(a) merely because of his being in an off-side position; or

(b) if he receives the ball direct from a goal-kick, a corner-kick or a throw-in.

4. If a player is declared off-side, the referee shall award an indirect free-kick, which shall be taken by a player of the opposing team from the place where the infringement occurred, unless the offence is committed by a player in his opponents' goal area, in which case the free-kick shall be taken from any point within the goal area.

Decisions of The International F.A. Board

(1) Off-side shall not be judged at the moment the player in question receives the ball, but at the moment when the ball is passed to him by one of his own side. A player who is not in an off-side position when one of his colleagues passes the ball to him or takes a free-kick, does not therefore become off-side if he goes forward during the flight of the ball.

2. A player who is level with the second last opponent or with the last two opponents is not in an off-side position.

9
Discipline

Physical and moral codes

Soccer was chosen by educationalists as a sport to strengthen bodies and to develop desirable qualities of character such as self-discipline, responsibility and a sense of justice.

Law XII allows for the game to be played in a robust but fair manner demanding physical effort while providing limits which enables players to exercise skills which they and others can enjoy.

The desired code of discipline is clear from the description of actions considered as misconduct in the third part of the law.

Law XII – Fouls and Misconduct

This law is the backbone of soccer. It provides the elements necessary to enable players to demonstrate their skills in a physical contact game within a code of conduct based on fair play to obtain the maximum of pleasure.

Fouls (unfair play) and misconduct, considered to be crimes against the intended method of play or the spirit of the game, are regulated by four punishments of varying degrees:

Indirect free-kick: for minor or technical offences;
Direct free-kick: for more serious offences;
Caution: an official warning against repetition of unfair play;
Dismissal: exclusion from the match.

The law can be separated into three parts: penal offences, technical offences and misconduct.

Penal Offences

The first part of the law lists nine offences for which a direct free-kick is awarded. They are usually referred to as penal offences because, if com-

Referees in action. Photo: Pro Sport

mitted by a defending player within his own penalty-area, the direct free-kick becomes a penalty-kick, a severe punishment which normally results in a goal. Law XIV describes the procedure for penalty-kicks.

Note the important qualification in the opening statement:

A player who INTENTIONALLY commits any of the following nine offences:

The offending player knows whether or not he intended to kick, push, hold or commit any of the other offences against an opponent but how can the referee be certain? Only by reading the clues in the manner in which the act was committed. Almost all referees have been players, and many still are. They understand the physical and emotional involvement and make judgements based on their own experience and feeling for fair play.

Eight of the nine offences concern actions against opponents. The ninth, handling the ball, contravenes the basic method of play decided over 100 years ago. This was a fundamental change from earlier games where hands could be used to control the ball.

The tradition was not easy to break. It is said that, to discourage converts to the game from handling, a group of enterprising ex-Harrow-School graduates provided players with white silk gloves and valuable silver

Penal offence: kicking an opponent

Tripping? Holding? or Fair? The referee must decide. Photo: Pro Sport

Destroyer of much skill, the deliberate tackle from behind is prohibited. A penal offence which can be punished by dismissal

Penal offence: jumping at an opponent

Penal offence: charging in a violent or dangerous manner

Who is holding? Who is pushing? Who should be punished? Photo: Presse Sports

Penal offence: holding. No doubt about intention here

Penal offence: handling the ball. A penalty-kick here and dismissal if the referee considers that the opponents have been denied an obvious goal-scoring opportunity (DECISION 16)

This is SERIOUS FOUL PLAY intended to destroy an obvious goal-scoring opportunity. The offender must be dismissed and a penalty-kick awarded if the offence occurred inside the penalty-area

Technical offence: Dangerous play

coins to be held in the hands during play. It is not recorded whether this practice was effective but there is no doubt that soccer became very popular in the Yorkshire area where it was introduced.

In recent years a trend towards deliberate handling, to deny opponents a clear goal-scoring opportunity, caused the International Board to decide, in 1991, that this offence should be classed as serious foul play requiring the referee to dismiss the offender (Decision 16).

This decision was a logical extension of another decision, announced in 1990, that a player who intentionally impedes an opponent and denies his team an obvious goal-scoring opportunity must be dismissed (Decision 15).

Technical Offences

The second part of Law 12 lists five offences punishable by an indirect free-kick. The first, dangerous play, covers any action which the referee considers dangerous to an opponent beyond the reasonable norm of danger to be expected in a physical contact sport. To the classical example quoted, attempting to kick the ball while held by the goalkeeper, can be added reckless challenges, overhead, or bicycle, kicks at the ball close to an opponent, etc.

Obstruction. When not playing the ball number 3

The second offence makes the point that charging with the shoulder, in order to put an opponent off-balance, can be fair but only when the ball is within playing distance. Playing distance means that the player can play the ball if he so wishes.

Obstruction, the third offence, is the intentional action of blocking the path of an opponent to deny a fair challenge for the ball. It also applies to attempts to prevent the goalkeeper from putting the ball into play (Decision 9).

The next paragraph provides protection for the goalkeeper against unfair charging. It used to be that legitimate goals could be scored by charging the goalkeeper into his own goal while holding the ball. Although the law (paragraph 4) allows a fair charge it is now rarely seen because protection has evolved to the point where goalkeepers have almost uncontested possession of the ball inside the whole of the penalty-area. This unintended freedom has led to tactics which exaggerated the role and influence of the goalkeeper to the detriment of attacking play.

Effectively, the ball is unplayable once in the hands of the goalkeeper. Paragraphs 5(a) and 5(b) are intended to encourage prompt release of the ball into play.

intentionally runs between the opponent and the ball. Indirect free-kick

To discourage the negative tactic of deliberately kicking the ball back into the goalkeeper's hands, by a defender under challenge, the International Board decided, in 1992, to remove the handling privilege in this situation and to punish any breach by the award of an indirect free-kick.

The message to goalkeepers is clear – you have protection to defend your goal but no right to excessive possession of the ball.

Misconduct

The final part of Law XII specifies punishments for offences against the code of behaviour required to maintain the game as a disciplined and honourable sport. If paragraphs (j), (k), (l) and (m) are converted into positive statements of the conduct expected from players they could read:

(j) understand that the referee must know at all times precisely who may be on the field to participate in the play.

(k) know the laws of the game to avoid offences.

(l) accept the referee's decisions without question.

(m) conduct yourself as a true sportsman.

Paragraph (m) refers to "ungentlemanly conduct", a reminder that the original soccer laws were prescribed for gentlemen players. A more modern expression would be "unsporting conduct" with the positive message to play with dignity and respect the true spirit of the game.

Paragraphs (n) and (o) state that any player who cannot control himself from committing acts of violent conduct, serious foul play or uses insulting language, must be dismissed.

The IB Decisions enlarge on basic law and describe certain offences with appropriate punishments. Decision 6 invokes the spirit of the laws by authorising the referee to delay disciplinary action in the interest of applying advantage as explained in the comments on Law V.

The referee indicates a "caution" by displaying a yellow card and a "dismissal" with a red card. Both punishments are reported to a competent authority (a league or organising body) for further action which may take the form of a fine or suspension from playing for a number of matches or a determined period.

An offence, which is not mentioned in the laws but which is important in relation to the desired code of conduct, is that of "bringing the game into disrepute". It covers any act which degrades the honour and good

Showing dissent, by word or action from any decision given by the referee. The player is cautioned and dismissed on further misconduct

reputation of soccer. Such acts are serious breaches of sporting etiquette.

Examples would include deliberate attempts to affect the results of matches by bribery, cheating or corruption. A specific case has been described in comments relative to Law VII. Administrators with responsibilities for protecting the good name of soccer, in addition to players, are subject to disciplinary measures if found guilty of this offence.

Summarising, this law incorporates the physical, ethical and moral codes necessary for players to take part in a healthy sport, to exercise personal skills within a team game for their own pleasure and that of others who watch them play.

LAW XII
Fouls and Misconduct

A player who intentionally commits any of the following nine offences:

(a) kicks or attempts to kick an opponent;

(b) trips an opponent, i.e. throwing or attempting to throw him by the use of the legs or by stooping in front of or behind him;

(c) jumps at an opponent;

(d) charges an opponent in a violent or dangerous manner;

(e) charges an opponent from behind unless the latter is obstructing;

(f) strikes or attempts to strike an opponent or spits at him;

(g) holds an opponent;

(h) pushes an opponent;

(i) handles the ball, i.e. carries, strikes or propels the ball with his hand or arm; (this does not apply to the goalkeeper within his own penalty-area);

shall be penalised by the award of a direct free-kick to be taken by the opposing team from the place where the offence occurred, unless the offence is committed by a player in his opponents' goal-area, in which case the free-kick shall be taken from any point within the goal area.

Should a player of the defending team intentionally commit one of the above nine offences within the penalty-area, he shall be penalised by a penalty-kick.

A penalty-kick can be awarded irrespective of the position of the ball, if in play, at the time an offence within the penalty-area is committed.

A player commiting any of the five following offences:

1. playing in a manner considered by the referee to be dangerous, e.g. attempting to kick the ball while held by the goalkeeper;

2. charging fairly, i.e. with the shoulder, when the ball is not within playing distance of the players concerned and they are definitely not trying to play it;

3. when not playing the ball, intentionally obstructing an opponent, i.e. running

between the opponent and the ball, or interposing the body so as to form an obstacle to an opponent;

4. charging the goalkeeper except when he:

(a) is holding the ball;

(b) is obstructing an opponent;

(c) has passed outside his goal-area.

5. when playing as a goalkeeper and within his own penalty-area:

(a) from the moment he takes control of the ball with his hands, he takes more than 4 steps in any direction whilst holding, bouncing or throwing the ball in the air and catching it again without releasing it into play, or,

(b) having released the ball into play before, during or after the 4 steps, he touches it again with his hands, before it has been touched or played by a player of the opposing team either inside or outside of the penalty area, or by a player of the same team outside the penalty area, subject to the overriding conditions of 5(c), or

(c) touches the ball with his hands after it has been deliberately kicked to him by a team-mate, or

(d) indulges in tactics which, in the opinion of the referee, are designed merely to hold up the game and thus waste time and so give an unfair advantage to his own team,

shall be penalised by the award of an **indirect free-kick** to be taken by the opposing side from the place where the infringement occurred, subject to the overriding conditions imposed in Law XIII.

A player shall be **cautioned** and shown the yellow card if:

(j) he enters or re-enters the field of play to join or rejoin his team after the game has commenced, or leaves the field of play during the progress of the game (except through accident) without, in either case, first having received a signal from the referee showing him that he may do so. If the referee stops the game to administer the caution, the game shall be restarted by an indirect free-kick taken by a player of the opposing team from the place where the ball was when the referee stopped the game, subject to the overriding conditions imposed in Law XIII.

If, however, the offending

player has committed a more serious offence, he shall be penalised according to that section of the law he infringed.

(k) he persistently infringes the Laws of the Game;

(l) he shows, by word or action, dissent from any decision given by the referee;

(m) he is guilty of ungentlemanly conduct.

For any of these last three offences, in addition to the caution, an **indirect free-kick** shall also be awarded to the opposing side from the place where the offence occurred, subject to the overriding conditions imposed in Law XIII, unless a more serious infringement of the Laws of the Game was committed.

A player shall be **sent off** the field of play and shown the red card, if, in the opinion of the referee, he:

(n) is guilty of violent conduct;

(o) is guilty of serious foul play;

(p) uses foul or abusive language;

(q) is guilty of a second cautionable offence after having received a caution.

If play is stopped by reason of a player being ordered from the field for an offence without a separate breach of the Law having been committed, the game shall be resumed by an **indirect free-kick** awarded to the opposing side from the place where the infringement occurred, subject to the overriding conditions imposed in Law XIII.

Decisions of The International F.A. Board

(1) If the goalkeeper either intentionally strikes an opponent by throwing the ball vigorously at him or pushes him with the ball while holding it, the referee shall award a penalty-kick, if the offence took place within the penalty-area.

(2) If a player deliberately turns his

back to an opponent when he is about to be tackled, he may be charged but not in a dangerous manner.

(3) In case of body contact in the goal-area between an attacking player and the opposing goalkeeper not in possession of the ball, the referee, as sole judge of intention, shall stop the game if, in his opinion, the action of the attacking player was intentional, and award an indirect free-kick.

(4) If a player leans on the shoulders of another player of his own team in order to head the ball, the referee shall stop the game, caution the player for ungentlemanly conduct and award an indirect free-kick to the opposing side.

(5) A player's obligation when joining or rejoining his team after the start of the match to "report to the referee" must be interpreted as meaning "to draw the attention of the referee from the touch-line". The signal from the referee shall be made by a definite gesture which makes the player understand that he may come into the field of play; it is not necessary for the referee to wait until the game is stopped (this does not apply in respect of an infringement of Law IV), but the referee is the sole judge of the moment in which he gives his signal of acknowledgement.

(6) The letter and spirit of Law XII do not oblige the referee to stop a game to administer a caution. He may, if he chooses, apply the advantage. If he does apply the advantage, he shall caution the player when play stops.

(7) If a player covers up the ball without touching it in an endeavour not to have it played by an opponent, he obstructs but does not infringe Law XII para. 3 because he is already in possession of the ball and covers it for tactical reasons while the ball remains within playing distance. In fact, he is actually playing the ball and does not commit an infringement; in this case, the player may be charged because he is in fact playing the ball.

(8) If a player intentionally stretches his arms to obstruct an opponent and steps from one side to the other, moving his arms up and down to delay his opponent, forcing him to change course, but does not make "bodily contact" the referee shall caution the player for ungentlemanly conduct and award an indirect free-kick.

(9) If a player intentionally obstructs the opposing goalkeeper, in an attempt to prevent him from putting the ball into play in accordance with Law XII, 5(a), the referee shall award an indirect free-kick.

(10) If, after a referee has awarded a free-kick, a player protests violently by using abusive or foul language and is sent off the field, the free-kick should not be taken until the player has left the field.

(11) Any player, whether he is within or outside the field of play, whose conduct is ungentlemanly or violent, whether or not it is directed towards an opponent, a colleague, the referee, a linesman or other person, or who uses foul or abusive language, is guilty of an offence, and shall be dealt with according to the nature of the offence committed.

(12) If, in the opinion of the referee a goalkeeper intentionally lies on the ball longer than is necessary, he shall be penalised for ungentlemanly conduct and

(a) be cautioned and an indirect free-kick awarded to the opposing team;

(b) in case of repetition of the offence, be sent off the field.

(13) The offence of spitting at officials and other persons, or similar unseemly behaviour shall be considered as violent conduct within the meaning of section (n) of Law XII.

(14) If, when a referee is about to caution a player, and before he has done so, the player commits another offence which merits a caution, the player shall be sent off the field of play.

(15) If, in the opinion of the referee, a player who is moving toward his opponent's goal with an obvious opportunity to score a goal is intentionally impeded by an opponent, through unlawful means, i.e. an offence punishable by a free-kick (or a penalty kick), thus denying the attacking player's team the aforesaid goalscoring opportunity, the offending player shall be sent off the field of play for serious foul play in accordance with Law XII (n).

(16) If, in the opinion of the referee, a player, other than the goalkeeper within his own penalty area, denies his opponents a goal, or an obvious goalscoring opportunity, by intentionally handling the ball, he shall be sent off the field of play for serious foul play in accordance with Law XII (n).

(17) The International F.A. Board is of the opinion that a goalkeeper, in the circumstances described in Law XII 5(a), will be considered to be in control of the ball by touching it with any part of his hands or arms. Possession of the ball would include the goalkeeper intentionally parrying the ball, but would not include the circumstances where, in the opinion of the referee, the ball rebounds accidentally from the goalkeeper, for example after he has made a save.

(18) Subject to the terms of Law XII, a player may pass the ball to his own goalkeeper using his head or chest or knee, etc. If, however, in the opinion of the referee, a player uses a deliberate trick in order to circumvent article 5(c) of Law XII, the player will be guilty of ungentlemanly conduct and will be punished accordingly under the terms of Law XII; that is to say, the player will be cautioned and shown the yellow card and an indirect free-kick will be awarded to the opposing team from the place where the player committed the offence.

In such circumstances, it is irrelevant whether the goalkeeper subsequently touches the ball with his hands or not. The offence is committed by the player in attempting to circumvent both the text and the spirit of Law XII.

10
Restarts

Simple procedures for restarting play

This final group of laws, XIII, XIV, XV, XVI and XVII, deals with the procedure of restarting the game after it has been stopped by the referee for an infringement or after the ball has crossed a boundary line.

An essential principle is to get the ball back into play in a simple fashion and with the minimum of delay. A common feature of these five laws, plus Law VIII, is that the player putting the ball into play is not allowed to touch it again until it has been touched by another player. He must release the ball and not run with it.

Law XIII – Free-kick

Hardly any soccer game is completed without free-kicks being awarded for offences of the nature described in the previous law. Numbers can vary according to the sporting attitude and conduct of the players. The 52 matches of the 1990 World Cup averaged 48 free-kicks with a low of 22 (Scotland v Costa Rica) and a high of 64 (Italy v Uruguay).

This law describes the conditions for the correct procedure for putting the ball into play after a free-kick is awarded.

There are two categories of free-kick:

a. Direct: a goal can be scored if the ball goes directly into the opponents' goal; and,
b. Indirect: a goal cannot be scored unless the ball is touched by a player other than the kicker.

For a direct free-kick, awarded for any of the penal offences listed in Law XII, the referee points the direction in which the kick shall be taken or to the penalty-spot if a defender has committed the offence inside his own penalty-area.

Direct Free-kick Signal

Indirect Free-kick Signal

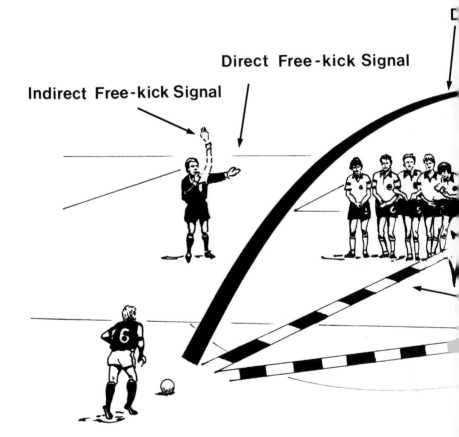

Free-kicks: direct and indirect

ee - kick — Goal

ect — Goal

To indicate that a free-kick is indirect the referee raises one arm above his head.

Definition: A FREE-KICK is the privilege of Kicking the Ball, without obstruction, in such a manner as the Kicker may think fit. (Original definition, 1863)

As a free-kick is intended to compensate the non-offending team for an offence committed by their opponents the definition provides for a FREE-FROM-OBSTRUCTION-KICK. In the law much emphasis is placed on the position of opposing players before the kick may be taken.

A frequent tactic in soccer is the formation of a "wall" of defenders between the ball and the goal. It is not illegal but any action intended to delay the kick or encroaching into the "free from obstruction" area, i.e. 10 yards radius from the ball, before the ball is kicked into play, is considered as a serious breach of fair play.

The problem is not new for the International Board issued a firm instruction to referees, in 1910, which now exists as Decision 2 after the law. It reads:

Players who do not retire to the proper distance when a free-kick is taken MUST be CAUTIONED and on any repetition ORDERED OFF.

The second sentence of this decision is also significant as it requires referees to treat delaying tactics as SERIOUS MISCONDUCT, a category of offence at least as grave as violent conduct or serious foul play listed in Law XII(n).

As already explained in Law V the referee may decide to allow a free-kick to be taken before the 10-yards limit is observed to deny the opposing team any advantage in delay. It is a practice to be encouraged in the interest of fair play.

A player cannot score a goal against his own side from a free-kick because the kick has been awarded to punish the offending team. Play is restarted with a corner-kick.

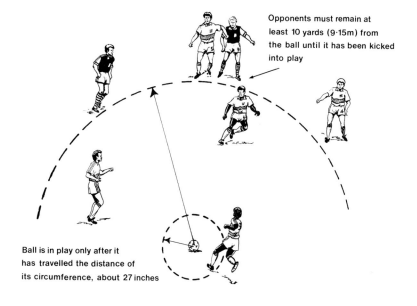

Opponents must remain at least 10 yards (9·15m) from the ball until it has been kicked into play

Ball is in play only after it has travelled the distance of its circumference, about 27 inches

Free kicks must not be obstructed by opponents. They must remain at least 10 yards (9.15 metres) from the ball until it has been kicked into play

The defensive 'wall'. Photo: Pro Sport

LAW XIII
Free-kick

Free-kicks shall be classified under two headings: "direct" (from which a goal can be scored direct against the offending side), and "indirect" (from which a goal cannot be scored unless the ball has been played or touched by a player other than the kicker before passing through the goal).

When a player is taking a direct or an indirect free-kick inside his own penalty-area, all of the opposing players shall be at least ten yards (9.15 metres) from the ball and shall remain outside the penalty-area until the ball has been kicked out of the area. The ball shall be in play immediately it has travelled the distance of its own circumference and is beyond the penalty-area. The goalkeeper shall not receive the ball into his hands, in order that he may thereafter kick it into play. If the ball is not kicked direct into play, beyond the penalty-area, the kick shall be retaken.

When a player is taking a direct or an indirect free-kick outside his own penalty-area, all of the opposing players shall be at least 10 yards from the ball, until it is in play, unless they are standing on their own goal-line, between the goal-posts. The ball shall be in play when it has travelled the distance of its own circumference.

If a player of the opposing side encroaches into the penalty-area, or within ten yards of the ball, as the case may be, before a free-kick is taken, the referee shall delay the taking of the kick, until the law is complied with.

The ball must be stationary when a free-kick is taken, and the kicker shall not play the ball a second time, until it has been touched or played by another player.

Notwithstanding any other reference in these Laws to the point from which a free-kick is to be taken:

1. Any free-kick awarded to the defending team, within its own goal-area, may be taken from any point within the goal-area.

2. Any indirect free-kick awarded to the attacking team within its opponent's goal-area shall be taken from the part of the goal-area line which runs parallel to the goal-line, at the point nearest to where the offence was committed.

Punishment

If the kicker, after taking the free-kick, plays the ball a second time before it has been touched or played by another player, an indirect free-kick shall be taken by a player of the opposing team from the spot where the infringement occurred, unless the offence is committed by a player in his opponent's goal-area, in which case, the free-kick shall be taken from a point within the goal-area.

Decisions of The International F.A. Board

(1) In order to distinguish between a direct and an indirect free-kick, the referee, when he awards an indirect free-kick, shall indicate accordingly by raising an arm above his head. He shall keep his arm in that position until the kick has been taken and retain the signal until the ball has been played or touched by another player or goes out of play.

(2) Players who do not retire to the proper distance when a free-kick is taken must be cautioned and on any repetition be ordered off. It is particularly requested of referees that attempts to delay the taking of a free-kick by encroaching should be treated as a serious misconduct.

(3) If, when a free-kick is being taken, any of the players dance about or gesticulate in a way calculated to distract their opponents, it shall be deemed ungentlemanly conduct for which the offender(s) shall be cautioned.

Law XIV – Penalty-kick

Just one penalty-kick can decide the whole of a soccer match, even the winner of a World Cup Final, as happened in the eighty-fifth minute of the 1990 final when Brehme converted from the penalty-mark for Germany against Argentina.

First introduced in 1891 the penalty-kick was intended to counter abuses by a growing number of professional players who employed any illegal means to prevent goals being scored. Deliberate handling was one of the main violations and the incident which finally convinced opponents to a penalty-kick occurred in an FA Quarter-Final match between Stoke City and Notts County early in 1891. Notts were leading 1–0 until the last minute when a defender punched the ball away as it was about to enter the goal. At that time the punishment was a free-kick which was awarded to Stoke near to the goal-line. The kick was blocked and Notts County won the match, subsequently to appear in the final where they lost to Blackburn Rovers.

Amateur players ignored the new law for some years considering that it applied only to paid players. They took the view that a penalty-kick awarded against their team was a slur on their moral behaviour to the point where the captain would instruct his goalkeeper to stand by a corner-post to leave the goal unprotected when the kick was taken.

Penalty-kick: introduced in 1891 to counter a 'professional foul'

Penalty-kick: not intended for 'gentleman' players!

The penalty-kick which won the 1990 World Cup Final for Germany against Argentina. Brehme puts the ball out of reach of goalkeeper Goyochea. Photo: Pro Sport

While sympathising with this ethical point of view the law makers insisted that the law must be enforced. Thus, it was amended to require the goalkeeper to stand on his goal-line "between the goal-posts".

The object of the law is to provide a punishment to fit the crime. One of the direct free-kick offences, listed in Law XII, has been committed and the team offended against should have a reasonable chance to redress the situation. However, a penalty-kick does not guarantee a goal – about 90% are converted – it becomes a test of skill between the kicker and the goalkeeper with the odds on the former. The interest is in how the two principal actors combat each other's skills.

The requirement that the goalkeeper must, "stand on his own goal-line . . . until the ball is kicked", was introduced in 1905 to cancel the goal-keeper's liberty to advance up to six yards towards the ball which had resulted in too many unsuccessful penalties. In 1929 a further restriction, to stop goalkeepers from moving laterally, was imposed so that now the goalkeeper must, "stand (without moving his feet) on his own goal-line".

The law is precise in the organisation of a penalty-kick and the decisions detail a number of procedures to be observed at infringements. Only the kicker and the goalkeeper are allowed inside the penalty-area, all other players must remain at least 10 yards from the ball and outside the penalty-area.

Careful supervision is required from the match officials to observe movement by the goalkeeper or encroachment by other players before the ball is kicked. As in other Laws the kicker must not play the ball a second time until it has been touched by another player.

The reason for extending time, to allow a penalty-kick to be completed, has been explained in comments on Law VII (Duration of the game). Decision 7, of Law XIV, states when the kick is considered to have been completed.

Penalty tie-breakers, or "shoot-outs", have become a feature of soccer in knock-out competitions where a match is drawn but a "winner" has to be determined to proceed to the next stage or receive a trophy in a final game. This procedure replaced the previous unsatisfactory ceremony, of tossing a coin or drawing lots, in 1970. "Shoot-outs" are not part of the match and do not nullify the criteria for deciding the result as laid down in Law X (Method of Scoring).

The special conditions to be met, at a penalty-kick ceremony, are that each team is allowed five kicks. The team "scoring" the most goals is declared the winner. If there is no result after the initial series of kicks the teams take alternative kicks until there is one goal difference after an equal number of attempts.

Both semi-finals of the 1990 World Cup were decided by the tie-breaker system.

LAW XIV
Penalty-kick

A penalty-kick shall be taken from the penalty-mark and, when it is being taken, all players with the exception of the player taking the kick, properly identified, and the opposing goalkeeper, shall be within the field of play but outside the penalty-area, and at least 10 yards from the penalty-mark. The opposing goalkeeper must stand (without moving his feet) on his own goal-line, between the goal-posts, until the ball is kicked. The player taking the kick must kick the ball forward; he shall not play the ball a second time until it has been touched or played by another player. The ball shall be deemed in play directly it is kicked, i.e. when it has travelled the distance of its circumference. A goal may be scored directly from a penalty-kick. When a penalty-kick is being taken during the normal course of play, or when time has been extended at half-time or full-time to allow a penalty-kick to be taken or retaken, a goal shall not be nullified if, before passing between the posts and under the cross-bar, the ball touches either or both of the goal-posts, or the cross-bar, or the goalkeeper, or any combination of these agencies, providing that no other infringement has occurred.

Punishment:

For any infringement of this law:

(a) by the defending team, the kick shall be retaken if a goal has not resulted;

(b) by the attacking team other than by the player taking the kick, if a goal is scored

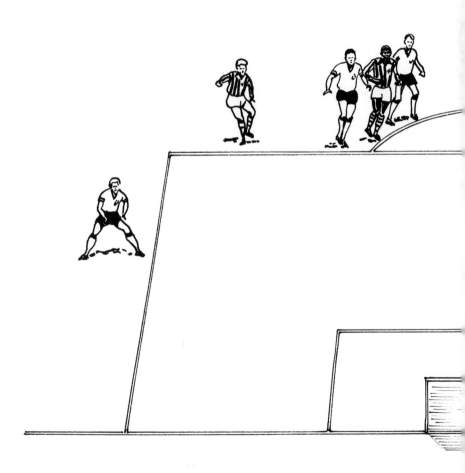

All players, except the kicker, must remain outside the penalty-area until the ball has been kicked into play. The goalkeeper must remain on his goal-line, between the posts

it shall be disallowed and the kick retaken;

(c) by the player taking the penalty-kick, committed after the ball is in play, a player of the opposing team shall take an indirect free-kick from the spot where the infringement occurred, subject to the over-riding conditions imposed in Law XIII.

Decisions of The International F.A. Board

(1) When the referee has awarded a penalty-kick, he shall not signal for it to be taken, until the players have taken up position in accordance with the Law.

(2) (a) If, after the kick has been taken, the ball is stopped in its course towards goal, by an outside agent, the kick shall be retaken.

(b) If, after the kick has been taken, the ball rebounds into play, from the goalkeeper, the cross-bar or a goal-post, and is then stopped in its course by an outside agent, the referee shall stop play and restart it by dropping the ball at the place where it came into contact with the outside agent, unless it was within the goal-area at that time, in which case it shall be dropped on the part of the goal-area line which runs parallel to the goal-line, at the point nearest to where the ball was when play was stopped.

(3) (a) If, after having given the signal for a penalty-kick to be taken, the referee sees that the goalkeeper is not in his right place on the goal-line, he shall, nevertheless, allow the kick to proceed. It shall be retaken, if a goal is not scored.

(b) If, after the referee has given the signal for a penalty-kick to be taken, and before the ball has been kicked, the goalkeeper moves his feet, the referee shall, nevertheless, allow the kick to proceed. It shall be retaken, if a goal is not scored.

(c) If, after the referee has given signal for a penalty-kick to be taken, and before the ball is in play, a player of the defending team encroaches into the penalty-area, or within ten yards of the penalty-mark, the referee shall, nevertheless, allow the kick to proceed. It shall be retaken, if a goal is not scored.

The player concerned shall be cautioned.

(4) (a) If, when a penalty-kick is being taken, the player taking the kick is guilty of ungentlemanly conduct, the kick, if already taken, shall be re-taken, if a goal is scored.

The player concerned shall be cautioned.

(b) If, after the referee has given the signal for a penalty-kick to be taken, and before the ball is in play, a col-league of the player taking the kick encroaches into the penalty-area or within 10 yards of the penalty-mark, the referee shall, nevertheless, allow the kick to proceed. If a goal is scored, it shall be disallowed, and the kick retaken.

The players concerned shall be cautioned.

(c) If, in the circumstances described in the foregoing paragraph, the ball rebounds into play from the goalkeeper, the cross-bar or a goal-post, and a goal has not been scored, the referee shall stop the game, caution the player and award an indirect free-kick to the opposing team from the place where the infringement occurred, subject to the overriding conditions imposed in Law XIII.

(5) (a) If, after the referee has given the signal for a penalty-kick to be taken, and before the ball is in play, the goalkeeper moves from his position on the goal-line, or moves his feet, and a colleague of the kicker encroaches into the penalty-area or within 10 yards of the penalty-mark, the kick, if taken, shall be retaken.

The colleague of the kicker shall be cautioned.

(b) If, after the referee has given the signal for a penalty-kick to be taken, and before the ball is in play, a player of each team encroaches into the penalty-area, or within 10 yards of the penalty-mark, the kick, if taken, shall

be retaken.

The players concerned shall be cautioned.

(6) When a match is extended, at half-time or full-time, to allow a penalty-kick to be taken or re-taken, the extension shall last until the moment that the penalty-kick has been completed, i.e. until the referee has decided whether or not a goal is scored, and the game shall terminate immediately the referee has made his decision.

After the player taking the penalty-kick has put the ball into play, no player other than the defending goalkeeper may play or touch the ball before the kick is completed.

(7) When a penalty-kick is being taken in extended time:

(a) the provisions of all of the foregoing paragraphs, except paragraphs (2) (b) and (4) (c) shall apply in the usual way, and

(b) in the circumstances described in paragraphs (2) (b) and (4) (c) the game shall terminate immediately the ball rebounds from the goalkeeper, the cross-bar or the goalpost.

Law XV – Throw-in

The number of throw-ins can vary from twenty, in a match played on a large field by skilled players, to nearly a hundred in a low-skill game played on a small field with difficult wind conditions.

Although the object is to get the ball back into play quickly and fairly a throw-in can have important tactical advantages. Some players develop skill in throwing the ball long distances. The two-handed throwing method was adopted in 1882 from a proposal of the Scottish FA. It replaced the one-handed method which was seen to be unfair when William Gunn, an English international, often propelled the ball the whole length of the field.

The one-handed throw-in gave an unfair advantage

The law is precise in describing the correct method of throwing-in. Any improper throw is punished by awarding a throw-in to the opposing team.

Remembering that off-side does not apply, a throw-in, taken in the opponents' half, can lead to a goal if the ball is thrown into the goal, although it must first be touched by another player. Should the ball pass directly into the goal the play is restarted with a goal-kick.

Sometimes a player will deliberately kick the ball over a touch-line in order to stop the game when another player appears to be seriously hurt. An interesting situation for the player is taking over the role of the referee whose duty it is to stop play for serious injury. The action is a considerate gesture of fair play which is invariably acknowledged in a practical manner by the team awarded the throw returning the ball immediately to their opponents.

Correct throw-in: 1 behind head, 2 over, 3 release. A continuous movement

Incorrect: a push-throw

Incorrect: both feet must remain on the ground, on or outside the touch-line

LAW XV
Throw-in

When the whole of the ball passes over a touch-line, either on the ground or in the air, it shall be thrown in from the point where it crossed the line, in any direction, by a player of the team opposite to that of the player who last touched it. The thrower at the moment of delivering the ball must face the field of play and part of each foot shall be either on the touch-line or on the ground outside the touch-line. The thrower shall use both hands and shall deliver the ball from behind and over his head. The ball shall be in play immediately it enters the field of play, but the thrower shall not again play the ball until it has been touched or played by another player. A goal shall not be scored direct from a throw-in.

Punishment:

(a) If the ball is improperly thrown in the throw-in shall be taken by a player of the opposing team.

(b) If the thrower plays the ball a second time before it has been touched or played by another player, an indirect free-kick shall be taken by a player of the opposing team from the place where the infringement occurred, subject to the overriding conditions imposed in Law XIII.

Decisions of The International F.A. Board

(1) If a player taking a throw-in plays the ball a second time by handling it within the field of play before it has been touched or played by another player, the referee shall award a direct free-kick.

(2) A player taking a throw-in must face the field of play with some part of his body.

(3) If, when a throw-in is being taken, any of the opposing players dance about or gesticulate in a way

calculated to distract or impede the thrower, it shall be deemed un-gentlemanly conduct, for which the offender(s) shall be cautioned.

(4) A throw-in taken from any posi-tion other than the point where the ball passed over the touch-line shall be considered to have been im-properly thrown in.

Law XVI – Goal-kick

Depending on conditions the number of goal-kicks in a soccer match can vary between ten and thirty. The average for the 1990 World Cup matches was eighteen.

Effectively, the attacking team has failed to score when one of its players puts the ball over the opponents goal-line outside the goal. Pos-session of the ball is lost to the defending team and it is put back into play by a kick from the goal-area. Although this task is often delegated to the goalkeeper it may be taken by any defender.

Goal-kicks are usually either long or short. Long kicks can be effective, particularly with a following wind, in putting the ball into the opponents' half to forwards who cannot be off-side from a goal-kick. A disadvantage is that there is a fifty-fifty chance of the ball going to an opponent.

If the ball is kicked directly into the opposite goal (quite a feat!) a goal will not be allowed. The opposing team will restart with a goal-kick.

Short kicks, to a defender standing outside the penalty-area, are usu-ally intended to retain possession to develop an attack.

The ball is not in play until it has passed outside the penalty-area.

LAW XVI
Goal-kick

When the whole of the ball passes over the goal-line ex-cluding that portion between the goal-posts, either in the air or on the ground, having last been played by one of the attacking team, it shall be kicked direct into play beyond the penalty-area from any point within the goal area by a player of the defending team. A goalkeeper shall not receive the ball into his hands from a goal-kick in order that he may thereafter kick it into play. If the ball is not kicked beyond the penalty-area, i.e. direct into play, the kick shall be re-taken. The kicker shall not play the ball a second time until it has touched or been played by another player. A goal shall not be scored direct from such a kick. Players of the team opposing that of the player taking the goal-kick shall remain outside the penalty-area until the ball has been kicked out of the penalty-area.

Punishment

If a player taking a goal-kick plays the ball a second time after it has passed beyond the penalty-area, but before it has touched or been played by another player, an indirect free-kick shall be awarded to the opposing team, to be taken from the place where the infringement occurred, subject to the overriding conditions imposed in Law XIII.

Decisions of The International F.A. Board

(1) When a goal-kick has been taken and the player who has kicked the ball touches it again before it has left the penalty-area, the kick has not been taken in accordance with the law and must be retaken.

Law XVII – Corner-kick

Although few in number, varying between four and fifteen (1990 World Cup average: nine), corner-kicks can be exciting because many players are usually positioned in the penalty-area. It is a fact that a goal often results from a corner-kick.

A corner-kick is a form of compensation for the attacking team when an opponent puts the ball, intentionally or accidentally, over his own goal-line outside of the goal. The kick is taken from the corner nearest to the point where the ball crossed the goal-line. The corner-quadrant limits the distance from the corner-post and provides enough space for the ball to be kicked without danger of injury from the post (which must not be removed).

Corner-kicks are opportunities for tactical innovation by attackers and defenders. Most corners are either long kicks into the goal-area or short passes to an attacker to tempt defenders away from goal or to mount an attack from an unexpected angle. With good skill the ball can be swerved into the goal directly for a valid goal or swerved away from the goal to avoid the hands of the goalkeeper and find a well positioned team-mate.

Off-side does not apply at corner-kicks, at the moment the ball is kicked, which allows attackers to position themselves on or close to the goal-line.

If the ball rebounds to the kicker from a goal-post, or the referee, it must not be played again by him until touched by another player. This point was overlooked by the referee when Tottenham played Huddersfield in an important league match in 1952. From a corner-kick the ball struck the referee, rebounded to the kicker who then passed it to a team-mate to score. The referee, probably dazed by the impact of the ball, awarded a goal. Tottenham won the match 1–0 and Huddersfield were relegated to the Second Division despite filing a formal protest to the Football League and requesting that the match be replayed.

A classic case of the referee being right even when proved wrong. Upholding this principle was considered more important than the interests of one club. One year after this incident Huddersfield won back promotion to the First Division.

Every corner-kick has potential for excitement and a goal

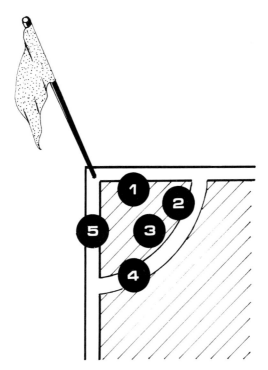

Placing the ball at a corner-kick: correct – 1, 2, 3; incorrect – 4, 5

Positions of players at a goal-kick: all players must remain outside the penalty-area until the ball leaves the area. Defenders may be in the area

Corner-kick: ball played a second time by the kicker, an error with serious consequences for Huddersfield Town

LAW XVII
Corner-kick

When the whole of the ball passes over the goal-line, excluding that portion between the goal-posts, either in the air or on the ground, having last been played by one of the defending team, a member of the attacking team shall take a corner-kick, i.e. the whole of the ball shall be placed within the quarter circle at the nearest corner-flagpost, which must not be moved, and it shall be kicked from that position. A goal may be scored direct from such a kick. Players of the team opposing that of the player taking the corner-kick shall not approach within 10 yards of the ball until it is in play, i.e. it has travelled the distance of its own circumference, nor shall the kicker play the ball a second time until it has been touched or played by another player.

Punishment

(a) If the player who takes the kick plays the ball a second time before it has been touched or played by another player, the referee shall award an indirect free-kick to the opposing team, to be taken from the place where the infringement occurred, subject to the overriding conditions imposed in Law XIII.

(b) For any other infringement the kick shall be retaken.

Law XVIII – Common sense

Definition: "Common sense: sound practical judgement."

"Law XVIII" is an unwritten law invented by referees to be applied in situations where the formal laws do not provide a clear answer to a specific problem. The referee is on his own to weigh up the unforeseen situation and apply sound practical judgement based on his interpretation of fair play and justice.

An actual example may serve to illustrate the point. A match is to be played on a field which is covered with stones, bottles and general refuse. In this state play would be dangerous. Assuming that there is no other field available nor assistance to clear the field the referee would be correct not to start the game. A possible solution would be to draw the attention of the two captains to the problem and suggest that both teams cooperate in clearing the field to a degree where the surface is acceptable to all.

Another example would be where a corner-post is broken during play and a replacement is not available. The referee would not abandon the match, because Law I insists on corner-posts, but would find some way of marking the corner with a visible object after informing the captains of the problem.

In both examples the prime object would be to conclude the matches with the cooperation of the players.

Fair Play in Sport

Definition

Fair Play is a code of conduct which respects not only the written but also the unwritten rules of the game and treats opponents as partners in sport.

Fair Play is expressed through spontaneous actions which applaud sporting excellence, show concern for opponents in distress, acknowledge defeat with dignity and victory with humility.

Sport with fair play enriches the quality of life.

The Fair Play Trophy, created by the French sculptor Jean Ipoustéguy, is inscribed 'mieux qu' une victoire' – 'better than a victory'

Chivalrous help at the final match
Italy – Germany FR in Madrid before the very eyes of the Brazilian referee

Glossary

Advantage:	An offence has been committed but the referee allows play to continue so that the offending team does not gain an advantage.
Attacker:	Any player in the opponents' half of the field.
Caution:	An official warning against continued misconduct or foul play. Indicated by the referee displaying a yellow card.
Centre-circle:	A circle of 10 yards (9.15 metres) radius drawn from a mark in the centre of the field.
Centre-mark:	A mark in the centre of the field from which Place-kicks are taken.
Charging:	Shoulder-to-shoulder contact to put an opponent off balance in order to obtain or retain possession of the ball.
Coach:	A team official who may convey tactical instructions to players during a match.
Corner-area:	The area contained within a quarter-circle of 1 yard (1 metre) radius drawn from each corner of the field.
Corner-kick:	A Direct free-kick taken from the corner-area after the ball has crossed the goal-line, outside of the goal, having been last touched by a player of the defending team.

Curtain Raiser:	A minor match played immediately before a major match, usually an international.
Dangerous Play:	Any act, which is not an intentional foul, considered by the referee to be dangerous to an opponent.
Defender:	Any player in his own half of the field.
Direct Free-kick:	A free-kick from which a goal may be scored if the ball goes directly into the goal unless taken by the defending team.
Drop-ball:	The ball is dropped by the referee to restart play after it has been stopped for a reason other than an offence by a player.
Extra-time:	An additional period of play to obtain a result after a match is drawn. Usually 30 minutes divided into two halves.
Fourth Official:	A substitute referee or linesman.
Free-kick:	Awarded for an offence by the opposing team. A kick at the ball free from obstruction by opponents. May be Direct or Indirect – see separate entries.
Goal:	The targets, comprising two upright posts and a joining cross-bar, placed at each end of the field through which the ball must pass to score a goal.
Goal-area:	An area, 6 × 20 yards (5.5 × 18.3 metres), marked in front of each goal.
Goalkeeper:	The only player in each team to have the privilege of handling the ball inside his own penalty-area. Dressed in colours to distinguish him from other players.
Goal-kick:	Method of restarting play after the ball has crossed the goal-line, outside of the goal, having been last touched by a player of the attacking team.
Goal-line:	The boundary line at each end of the field on which the goals are placed.
Half-way Line:	A line drawn across the centre of the field.

Hand Ball: An offence when a hand or any part of an arm, up to the shoulder joint, is used with the intention of touching the ball.

Holding: Intentional use of the arms to physically obstruct an opponent.

Indirect Free-kick: A free-kick from which a goal cannot be scored direct. The ball must touch a player, other than the kicker, before a goal can be scored.

International FA Board: The governing body for the Laws of the Game.

Jumping at an Opponent: An offence when a player jumps at an opponent intentionally to prevent him from playing the ball.

Kick-off: A Place-kick, taken from the centre of the field to start the game, to restart after half-time and after each goal is scored.

Linesman: An assistant to the referee with a patrol outside a touch-line who signals, with a flag, when the ball has crossed a boundary line and undertakes any other duties delegated by the referee.

Misconduct: Any act of misbehaviour contrary to the letter and spirit of the Laws of the Game.

National Association: The recognised governing body for soccer in the country concerned.

Obstruction: An offence when a player, who is not playing the ball, intentionally runs between an opponent and the ball or interposes his body to form an obstruction.

Off-side: An offence when a player, in an off-side position, is considered by the referee to be interfering with play or an opponent.

Off-side Position: A player is in an off-side position if he is nearer to his opponents' goal-line than the ball unless: (a) he is in his own half, or (b) he has at least two opponents either level with him or nearer to the goal-line.

Outside Agency: Any agency which is not part of the game.

Penalty-arc: An arc drawn outside the penalty-area with a radius of 10 yards (9.15 metres) from the penalty-mark. It indicates the minimum distance from the ball which must be observed by all players at a penalty-kick excepting the kicker and goalkeeper.

Penalty-area: An area, 18 × 44 yards (16.5 × 40.3 metres), marked in front of each goal.

Penalty-mark: The place from which penalty-kicks are taken 12 yards (11 metres) from the mid-point of the goal-line.

Place-kick: A kick at the ball while it is stationary on the ground in the centre of the field. See also Kick-off.

Referee: An official appointed to supervise and control a game usually assisted by two linesmen.

Result: The team scoring the greater number of goals is the winner; if no goals or an equal number of goals are scored, the game is a "draw".

Serious Foul-play: Usually applies to any of the direct free-kick offences, listed in Law XII, being committed in a serious manner.

Substitute: A non-participating player who may be called upon to replace a participating player.

Throw-in: The method of restarting play when the ball has passed out of bounds over a touch-line.

Tie-breaker: A system used to determine the winning team when a match is drawn in a knock-out competition. It comprises a series of kicks from the penalty-mark.

Touch-line: The boundary line at each side of the
                             field.

Tripping an Opponent: Bringing down, or attempting to bring
                             down, an opponent by the use of the legs
                             or by stooping in front of or behind him.

Violent Conduct: Any violent act of a physical or moral
                             nature.

Questions and Answers to The Laws of the Game

A selection of official questions from National Associations together with answers approved by The International Football Association Board.

Law I – The Field of Play

Q. For a corner-kick, is it permitted to mark the nearest distance which must be kept by players of the opposing team?

A. Yes, if it is marked outside the field of play, at right angles and at a specific distance from the goal-line and touch-line respectively and at 9.15 metres (10 yards) from the edge of the quarter-circle.

Q. If a goalkeeper draws unauthorised marks on the field of play with his foot, what action should the referee take?

A. If the referee notices that this is being done during the match, he need not interrupt the game just to caution the player who is making unauthorised marks on the field of play after the match has started. The player concerned must be cautioned for ungentlemanly conduct when there is an interruption in the game. If, however, the referee notices this before the match starts, then he shall caution the offending player immediately.

Law III – Number of Players

Q. If a player in possession of the ball passes over the touch-line, or the goal-line, without the ball in order to beat an opponent, should the referee penalise him for leaving the field of play without permission?

A. No. Going outside the field of play may be considered as part of a playing movement, but players are expected, as a general rule, to remain within the playing area.

Q. May an expelled player stay on the substitutes bench?

A. No. An expelled player shall return to the dressing room.

Q. Is a substitute considered to be a member of the team at the moment he enters the field of play or when the referee restarts the game?

A. The substitution is completed when the substitute enters the field of play, provided the game has been stopped, the player being replaced has left the field and the referee has signalled his permission for the substitute to enter the field of play at the half-way line.

Law IV – Players' Equipment

Q. If a player, following doctor's orders, protects his elbow or any similar part of his body with a bandage to prevent further injury, has the referee the power to decide if the bandage constitutes a danger to other players?

A. Yes.

Q. If the colour of the shirts of the two goalkeepers is the same, what should the referee do if neither has another shirt to change into?

A. The referee shall allow play to continue.

Law V – Referees

Q. Is the referee empowered to order team officials away from the boundary lines of the field of play?

A. Yes, the referee has the right to take such measures even if the match is being played on a public ground.

Q. Does a team captain have the right to question a decision of the referee?

A. No, neither the captain nor any other player has the right to show disagreement with a decision taken by the referee.

Law VII – Duration of the Game

Q. Is it left to the referee's discretion to decide whether lost time (injuries or other causes) are to be compensated or not?

A. No, the referee must add on in each half of the game all time lost. However, the amount of such time is at the discretion of the referee.

Law VIII – The Start of Play

Q. If the ball is kicked straight into the opponents' goal from the kick-off, what decision does the referee give?

A. Goal-kick to the opposing team.

Q. Is the ball out of play if any part of the ball overlaps either the goal-line or the touch-line?

A. No, the whole of the ball must cross the line.

Q. The ball accidentally hits the referee or a linesman on the field of play and rebounds into goal. What should the referee's decision be?

A. The referee shall award the goal.

Law X – Method of Scoring

Q. If a referee signals a goal before the ball has passed wholly over the goal-line and he immediately realises his error, is the goal valid?

A. No. The game shall be restarted by dropping the ball on that part of the goal-area line, parallel to the goal-line, nearest to the place where it was when the referee inadvertently stopped play.

Law XI – Off-side

Q. Does a player infringe the law if he is in an off-side position and moves a little way beyond the boundary of the field of play to show clearly to the referee that he is not interfering with play?

A. No, but if the referee considers that such a move has a tactical aim or is in any way a feint, and the player takes part in the game immediately after, the referee may deem his action to be ungentlemanly conduct and caution him. Play shall be restarted in accordance with the Laws of the Game.

Q. What action should the referee take if a defending player moves beyond his own goal-line in order to place an opponent in an off-side position?

A. The action of the defender is considered as ungentlemanly conduct, but it is not necessary for the referee to stop play immediately to caution the player. The attacker should not be punished for the position in which he has been unfairly placed.

Law XII – Fouls and Misconduct

Q. What action should the referee take if a player of the defending team, other than the goalkeeper, standing outside the penalty-area, intentionally handles the ball within the penalty-area?

A. He shall penalise the player by awarding the penalty-kick because the offence took place within the penalty-area.

Q. If a referee cautions a player who in turn apologises for his misconduct, can the referee omit to report the incident?

A. No, all cautions must be reported.

Q. What action should the referee take against players who leave the field while celebrating a goal?

A. Celebrating a goal is all part of football. A caution is only warranted if a player gives an excessive demonstration of jubilation, e.g. by jumping over the boundary fence, gesticulating at his opponents or the spectators or ridiculing them by pointing to his shirt.

Q. How should a player be penalised for throwing an object (stone, shoe) or spitting from within the penalty-area at a player who is outside the penalty-area?

A. He must be penalised by a penalty-kick and be sent off.

Q. Is there a difference in the punishment to be given for spitting at an opponent or attempting to do so?

A. No. Spitting or attempting to do so are equally grave offences.

Law XIII – Free-kick

Q. When taking a free-kick awarded to their team, may players use feinting tactics to confuse opponents?

A. Yes. Furthermore, if the opponents move nearer than 9.15 metres (10 yards) to the ball before it is in play, they shall be cautioned.

Q. A player wishes to play a free-kick quickly with an opponent being only 4.5 metres from the ball. Should the referee allow this?

A. Yes, and even if an opponent intercepts the ball, play shall be allowed to continue.

Law XIV – Penalty-kick

Q. If a penalty-kick is retaken because the goalkeeper moved his feet, must the same player take the kick again or could another player do so?

A. Another player could also retake the penalty-kick.

Q. If a player takes a penalty-kick before the referee has signalled, what action should the referee take?

A. The kick must be retaken. The player shall be cautioned only if he takes the penalty-kick again without awaiting the referee's signal.

Q. Does taking kicks from the penalty-mark to determine the winner of a match form part of the match?

A. Such kicks from the penalty-mark never form part of a match.

Law XV – Throw-in

Q. Is there a maximum distance away from the touch-line from which a throw-in may be taken?

A. No. A throw-in should be taken from the place where the ball left the field of play. However, a distance of up to one metre from the exact position is a common practical guideline.

Q. If an opponent stands in front of a player at a throw-in to impede him, what action should the referee take?

A. Allow the throw-in to be taken if the opponent remains stationary. But if he moves or gesticulates to distract the thrower, he shall be cautioned for ungentlemanly conduct.

Law XVI – Goal-kick

Q. If a player is intentionally tripped before the ball passes outside of the penalty-area when a goal-kick is being taken, should a free-kick be awarded?

A. No, the ball is not in play until it has been out of the penalty-area. The offender shall be cautioned or sent off and the goal-kick retaken.

A booklet containing over 150 official Questions and Answers, including the foregoing, is available from FIFA.